LEADING
AT THE SPEED
OF PEOPLE

LEADING AT THE SPEED OF PEOPLE

Strategies for Success in a Fast-Paced World

JULIE DONLEY, EDD, MBA, RN, PCC

First Printing 2024

Formatter: Heru Setiawan

Cover design: Jeanly Zamora

Editor: Robin Reed

ISBN: 978-0-9765605-8-6 (Paperback)
ISBN: 978-0-9765605-7-9 (Hardcover)
ISBN: 978-0-9765605-2-4 (Ebook)

Contents

Preface

For many years, I aspired to write a book on leadership, knowing that eventually, I would. Timing is everything. I needed to find the time, of course, but I also needed to develop and refine my ideas and perspective on the topic. Once I achieved my doctorate and stepped away from my leadership role, I was able to fully focus on coaching leaders and create the space needed to write this book.

Initially, I referred to it as *The Leadership Book*. Drawing from my years of experience, education, and understanding of people and effective leadership, I aimed to write about what makes for a good leader and how we become effective in our leadership roles. Given today's fast-paced, changing landscape, with the rise of artificial intelligence, civil unrest, and widespread burnout and stress, loneliness, substance abuse, and all the other global challenges we are facing, we need to transform our approach to leadership. We seem to have lost our way and need a new vision, adjusting our leadership strategies to the times.

Leadership is fundamentally about serving the people we lead and eliciting their best efforts, and it begins with leading ourselves. As you will learn in the book, leading is about connecting—forming relationships, influencing others, and becoming the type of person others want to follow.

In crafting the title, I wanted something that encapsulated this essence. From understanding people by tapping into our own humanity, to my lessons of respect and empathy from decades of working in behavioral health, and even a section on trauma-informed leadership, finding the right title was challenging.

Ultimately, this book teaches two major activities for leaders to focus their attention and efforts while better understanding people and how they operate: reducing friction and connecting. Reducing friction involves lessening or eliminating stressors where possible and removing obstacles so people can perform at their best.

For connecting, I offer the acronym CARE: Communicate, Appreciate, Respect, and Empathize. These elements are crucial for leaders to connect with their teams effectively. Leading with respect, empathy, and appreciation unlocks the potential within employees, allowing them to unleash their creativity and intelligence.

People want to unleash their greatness; they just need the support, encouragement, and the right environment to access their greatness. Leaders are uniquely positioned to help with that.

To rediscover what it means to lead effectively amidst changing priorities and fast-paced demands, we must reexamine our current approaches and redefine our style to match the needs of the day. It starts with relearning what it means to be human in today's world. Leadership today requires a renewed emphasis on humanity, values, and empathy, understanding that people carry significant emotional stress and pain. We must shift our focus from merely getting things done to truly understanding and supporting the people who do the work—who they are, what they need, their challenges, hopes, desires, and strengths. Our goal is to help others become more of what they are capable of in today's world.

The title *Leading at the Speed of People* invites us to reconsider the pace at which we lead. In our quest for productivity, are we speeding through the essential human elements of leadership? Leading people effectively requires a different approach than merely accomplishing tasks. This book aims to help leaders adopt a people-first mentality, prioritizing well-being and creating a more engaged, impactful workforce. And maybe, we can enjoy the journey along the way.

Introduction

Leadership is an art form, a dance. It is the delicate interaction between doing our work, connecting with others, and managing ourselves to produce the outcomes we desire.

As we step into leadership roles, we embark on a journey of self-discovery. We find our voice, advocate for what we believe in, overcome obstacles, and confront our internal challenges. We face our fears, engage in crucial conversations, and navigate conflicts. Through this process, we stretch, grow, and evolve as human beings.

Leading requires much from us, yet we often learn to lead through trial and error. We read books, observe other leaders, and experiment with different approaches, adjusting and refining our methods as we go.

Research has shown that many people leave their jobs in search of greater pay, but beyond financial compensation, leaders play a crucial role in meeting higher-level needs for safety, belonging, esteem, and purpose. Leaders have the power to create environments where people can thrive, ensuring that their basic needs are met and providing opportunities for growth and fulfillment.

Despite this, many leaders have not developed the skills necessary to make a meaningful impact. We do the best we can as we fumble to figure things out, and yet there must be a better way of developing leaders so they know what is expected, how to take a stand, and what they could and should be doing to ensure that people have a positive experience at work. Too much time is wasted trying to figure out an approach to leading. I hope to change that with this book. Ineffective leadership is costly and stressful, and more difficult than it needs to be. When leadership is ineffective, it contributes to high turnover, absenteeism, low morale, and disengagement, all of which are costly to organizations.

While some things are out of our control, there is plenty we have control over, and finding our power and our voice is essential for ensuring we are doing what we can to support and develop our employees. For example, we can encourage and support creativity, work to unleash potential, and provide psychological safety, but we cannot force someone to rise to the challenge, become more confident, and experience purpose and meaning in their work. Each of us must do the inner work to become a better human, to face our fears, to be brave and tackle our "mind muck"—the inner thoughts, habits, and beliefs that hold us back from being brilliant and shining brightly.

In this book we will explore the elements of effective leadership. In Part I, we delve into the foundations of good and bad leadership, helping you define what effective leadership means for you, and highlighting the importance of self-leadership.

In Part II, we shift our focus to strategies that enable leaders to add value, find their power, and reduce friction, creating a respectful and healthy work environment where employees can thrive. We uncover ways to reduce stress and work more efficiently by making work life easier for everyone involved. Corporate life is messy, and as leaders we must learn how to stop contributing to that messiness! By taking an inside-out approach, we begin to explore ourselves and unpack how we may be getting in the way. Awareness brings choice, and choice gives us power.

In Part III, we concentrate on the keys to connecting and building positive, healthy relationships. Leadership is a people's game. It begins with leading yourself—becoming more self-aware, confident, empowered, and compassionate. Then, it extends to leading others with respect and empathy, helping them develop and succeed.

We have come to accept a stressful way of working as normal. We are so accustomed to this way of work that many of us don't know anything different—this is our baseline! Many of us don't know what it's like to be respected and valued at work, or to have our well-being prioritized. It doesn't have to be this way. As leaders, we have the power to change this. We can create workplaces where people feel understood, safe, and cared for.

This book is the culmination of my thirty-year career, filled with insights and practical strategies for leading well. Throughout this book, I share stories from my work in behavioral healthcare. The lessons I learned about people's basic human needs for respect, kindness, and care have shaped my leadership strategies. My experiences with both ineffective and effective leaders have driven me to study leadership and to strive for excellence in my own leadership journey.

This book is the fruit of my labor to uncover the truth about leadership. I hope you enjoy reading it as much as I enjoyed writing it. I look forward to hearing about your experiences and how this book has helped you grow in confidence and reduce your stress.

Respectfully yours,

Dr. Julie Donley

PART I

The Making of
a Leader

*Taking on a challenge is a lot like riding a
horse, isn't it? If you're comfortable while you're
doing it, you're probably doing it wrong.*

—TED LASSO

S tepping up into leadership takes courage. While some people
may be naturally inclined to lead, leaders are shaped through
their experiences.

In this section of the book, we tackle the challenges of leadership,
examine the costs of ineffective leadership, and introduce the elements
of effective leadership. I suggest you keep a journal where you can
reflect on yourself and your leadership approaches and identify
strategies to experiment with, so you can grow in your leadership as
you read through the book.

Leading others begins with self-exploration. If you are to lead
others, you start by leading yourself. You are the curriculum for

1

learning about people and what it means to be human. Leadership is all about relationships—relating to other people. So naturally, that begins by relating to yourself.

Understanding what it takes to effectively lead others starts with imagining what you want for yourself and your department (or area of responsibility) and then defining the qualities of the kind of leader you want to be. While there is a lot that I can share with you about the research on effective leadership and its elements, you must adapt everything to suit your style, your personality, and the context within which you work. This self-exploration is necessary for guiding your actions and your approach to leading others.

CHAPTER 1

Stepping Up into Leadership

> *Before you are a leader, success is all about growing yourself. When you become a leader, success is all about growing others.*
>
> —JACK WELCH

It was a new leadership role for my coaching client. When we started working together, she declared that she was entirely too busy, taking on way too much work, and not taking time for herself or her family. She was quickly burning out. To better her chances of success, she enrolled in a leadership course, although it would mean added work. The course included leadership coaching, and she chose to work with me as her coach.

Initially, we discussed her goals for our time together. The conversations then moved to uncovering what she believed about being a leader as opposed to being an individual contributor. The work of a professional coach is to help clients unpack the beliefs, assumptions, and thinking that drive the person to behave as they do. This sheds light on their perspective, mindset, and habits of thought, so they can make better, more effective choices about who they want to be and how they want to behave. For this client, there was guilt (about taking time off or delegating work), perfectionism, concern about being seen as lazy, concern about not being available—lots of thinking that was not supporting her efforts to lead, but rather keeping her busy, stressed, and unhappy.

Many leaders get caught in a web of thinking that serves as noise and distracts them from leading. This thinking does not serve them to actually *lead*, but rather pushes them to (attempt to) be all things to all people, to question and doubt themselves, or to do it all themselves. They get lost in the noise in their heads. This results in stress, overwhelm, dissatisfaction, and burnout. And this means they don't *lead*; they work harder and harder and (try to) please others, do it all, and do it all perfectly. This thinking fails us.

Good Employee? Let's Promote You

When did you know you wanted to lead? What was the driving force that motivated you to choose to become a leader? Some leaders choose to step up into leadership to stretch themselves, wanting to make a difference and a bigger contribution. They look forward to influencing their team to achieve organizational goals. Others fall into the role either because no one else is willing or able to step up or they get promoted because they are skilled professionals. Which were you? How did you get here? And what is important to you about leading?

Whatever path you took to step up into leadership, once you are here, you quickly learn that there are skills necessary to navigate this new landscape. The skills that helped you become top in your field are not the same skills needed to effectively lead other people. And with each level you climb in leadership, you will need additional skills in order to be effective.

Organizations often do not provide sufficient onboarding into new roles or provide leadership development training. There is often the assumption that you will just figure it out. You are expected to step into the new role, know just what to do, and get started making everything better. At any level of leadership, this can be challenging. It can be especially daunting if you are new to leading!

The number one way that people learn how to lead is trial and error. And let's face it, each of us has to find our own path to leading effectively, so trial and error will be part of our learning process. We each have our own style, personality, education, and experience, which we then have to sculpt to the context.

Besides trial and error, we study leadership, read lots of books, and watch others. We learn from bad leaders, and we learn from good leaders. We study and observe and experience. If we are lucky, we learn from mentors and have access to a coach. Then we need to do our best, practice, and learn from our actions through regular reflection.

When leaders are promoted to any level and are ill-equipped, this can result in leaders who are ineffective and may not even know it. If you are learning from others around you and there is a culture that promotes a certain type of leadership, you can adopt some bad habits and not realize that there is another way. "How things are done around here" is a mindset and thinking pattern that can be repeated without questioning and discernment.

The problem compounds when we are promoted without the essential skill development and access to leadership resources such as mentors, coaches, or leadership development training. We don't know what we don't know. Organizations that provide resources to help lessen the learning curve benefit greatly. Without sufficient instruction and direction, not only can we be ineffective, but we can also become stressed-out, and our behaviors directly affect our employees, our team, the organization, and the bottom line, as well as the community at large.

Stressed-Out! The Current State of Work

The rush and pressure of modern life . . . is
perhaps the most common form of contemporary
violence. To allow oneself to be carried away by
a multitude of conflicting concerns, to surrender
to too many demands, to commit oneself to

> *too many projects, to want to help everyone*
> *and everything is to succumb to violence.*

—THOMAS MERTON

The way we are working is not working. In a recent article by Gallup, 44 percent of employees worldwide report being stressed—a figure that has risen consistently over the past decade.[1] Numerous articles and books in the last few years speak to the stress and burnout we are experiencing because of how we approach our work. It seems that each day there is a new podcast episode, article, or research study on stress, trauma, and the impact they are having on our lives. That in and of itself is overwhelming!

In his book *Dying for a Paycheck*, Jeffery Pfeffer shares that workplace stress is actually the fifth-leading cause of death in the United States.[2] We seem to be doing something wrong. If work is killing us, then we must figure out different ways to approach it—it's literally a matter of life and death!

This is not a new phenomenon; it's just evolved to the point where we can no longer ignore our reality. We seem to have developed a mindset where busyness and money are the values by which we measure success above all else, and the only path to achieving that is to nurture an unsustainable intensity around our ability to deliver at work. If this is how we think about it, then we will continue to create and recreate it. To create a new culture of work, we need a new way of thinking about work and leadership.

For decades people have focused on creating work environments that are safer for workers. In the 1960s, the occupational health movement grew from a need to provide adequate safety interventions to protect workers from environmental hazards and work practices that created dangerous working conditions. Over the years, much research has been done on the physical effects of work as well as the psychosocial aspects of the work environment and their impact on worker health and well-being.[3] The stress and strain of work has been linked to physical issues, including heart disease, obesity, and various forms of cancer, and mental health issues such as depression, anxiety, and even suicide. The costs in terms of absenteeism, turnover, and lost productivity are estimated in the billions of dollars annually.[4]

People often think of occupational health practices as providing safety policies and protocols related to physical health and injury prevention; however, the psychological aspects of work are important as well. Stress at work increases in response to unsafe working conditions and also to unsafe social situations where people are unhappy, are not treated fairly, lack autonomy, and lack recognition. In her research, Amy Edmonson identified that psychological safety is essential for healthy teams and for collaboration, innovation, and individual risk-taking, and that the lack of psychological safety increased people's stress and inability to show up fully at work.[5] Not having a voice at work, not being heard or seen or valued, not being able to be yourself, but rather having to cover up or shrink—all increase the stress experienced at work. When employees do not feel safe, respected, or appreciated, their performance suffers, and the organization pays the price.

The social aspects of work cannot be understated. According to the Surgeon General of the United States, Vivek Murthy, loneliness has become an epidemic, and studies show that a best friend at work can mitigate loneliness, depression, and despair.[6] In fact, studies show that relationships are one of the main reasons people remain in their jobs.[7] What has happened that we are so isolated at work, and we feel so separated and lonely? Loneliness is stressful.

In 2019 the World Health Organization (WHO) identified burnout in the International Classification of Diseases (ICD-11) not as a medical condition, but rather as an occupational phenomenon.[8] This means that burnout is understood to result from work situations where "chronic workplace stress has not been successfully managed." It is characterized by three dimensions: feelings of energy depletion or exhaustion, cynicism, and reduced professional efficacy. If burnout occurs because of how we are managing the stress we experience at work, that means we can learn ways to approach work differently.

So, what causes burnout? In studies conducted by the Gallup organization, they identified the top five causes as unfair treatment at work, an unmanageable workload, unclear communication from managers, lack of manager support, and unreasonable time pressure.[9] Numerous studies over the last fifty years have shown that as job demands rise, stress and strain increase. Studies on employee outcomes such as employee engagement and job satisfaction have demonstrated that dissatisfaction at work leads to stress, burnout, and turnover.

What we conclude from this information is that leaders directly impact how people work, which means that we can adapt how we work, how we treat people in the workplace, and how we get work done, so people can have a different experience at work. Leaders play a key role in creating and maintaining a healthy work environment where psychological safety is a priority. This means fostering open communication, encouraging collaboration, and recognizing and valuing each team member's contributions.

John Maxwell, author and leadership expert, states that "everything rises and falls with leadership." Leaders often place unrealistic pressures on themselves, they experience a lot of pressure from others within the organization, and there are outside pressures as well, from family stressors to global stressors. As a leader you play an important role in your employees' lives, and you make a big impact— positively or negatively. When you are stressed-out, that directly impacts the people with whom you work, and then you take that stress home with you and out into the community.

You may have received the wrong message about leading— what you think you are supposed to do and how you are supposed to do it may be causing you angst and adding to your stress. One woman shared with me that she had worked diligently to rise in her organization and become an executive. After only a year in the role, just when she reached the pinnacle of her career, she got so burned-out that she had to take a sabbatical. Through her healing and time of self-reflection, she learned that she had received the wrong message about leading and was practicing her leadership in a way that essentially cost her the career she thought she wanted and had worked so hard for. She has since found other employment and approaches work much differently. She enjoys a great life today, so the lessons were beneficial, but they came at a high cost.

We don't have to have all the answers, we don't need to do it all, and we don't need to be perfect, yet in our quest to do great work, we stress out and burn out. The alarm has sounded. It is time to wake up.

The way forward involves rethinking how we approach work and leadership, prioritizing the well-being of employees, and creating a culture that values human connection and psychological safety. By doing so, we can reduce stress, improve productivity, and create a more sustainable and fulfilling work environment for everyone.

The Shift: A New Approach to Leadership

What got you here won't get you there.

— MARSHALL GOLDSMITH

If we want different results, we need to think new thoughts, and that requires a shift in mindset. Shifts are often uncomfortable, and yet we know that the thinking that got us here won't get us where we want to go. If we want to thrive at work and have a great life while leading, then we must approach our work and leadership differently. And if we want to be an inspiration and role model for others, help them thrive at work, and create high-performing teams and organizations, then we must think differently about the way we work and the environment we create within which our employees work.

In their work on what motivates people at work, Richard Ryan and Edward Deci developed the self-determination theory (SDT). SDT identified that people have basic human needs for autonomy, competence, and relatedness, and they feel motivated to act when those needs are fulfilled.[10] People are motivated to act either due to external rewards and motivators or intrinsic motivation. Intrinsic motivation comes from the person's desire to act because it feels good and brings personal satisfaction.

The psychological needs identified in SDT support an individual's psychological well-being and sense of optimal functioning. With autonomy, people can self-govern, have control over their work, and function to the degree that they have capacity and knowledge. Competence enables that person to perform with minimal oversight and practice their craft to the best of their ability. And relatedness is the basic human need for connection. Relationships provide personal satisfaction and well-being, and connecting and being part of a group is a mitigating factor for loneliness, dissatisfaction at work, and mental health concerns.

Much research has been done over the years regarding motivation at work and what leads to employee outcomes. We know what makes people satisfied and engaged at work. Why does it seem so hard for us to do what we know works?

In his book *Three Signs of a Miserable Job*, Patrick Lencioni identified irrelevance, immeasurability, and anonymity as telltale signs that you are not in a good work environment.[11] People want to be seen, heard, and valued; they don't want to be invisible. People need to know that their job matters and that their work is valued; they want to be relevant and connect with the larger purpose of the organization. People also want to have their work measured in some way, so they can see how they have progressed, the impact they have had, and how they can continue to develop themselves and make an impact.

My interest in this topic extended to my dissertation research. In studying the psychosocial work environment and the factors that lead to satisfaction at work, I read hundreds of empirical research papers as well as completed a research project of my own.[12] The answers are clear: People want to be appreciated, supported, developed, and valued. They want to be treated with respect, to work in a community (teams, groups, collaboration) where they can perform their best work, be acknowledged for their work, find meaning in their work, and enjoy their work. People want work that is consistent and organized, where there are clear instructions and expectations; where job demands are appropriate to the resources available; and where individual needs for interpersonal relations are met—that someone at work takes time to get to know them and cares about them as a human being.

If we want to create a new culture of work, then we must do things differently. And that starts with looking inward at how we lead ourselves.

Start Here: The Role of Self-Leadership

*The most important singular thing that each one
of us possesses is himself. Each of us is given to
himself and our task in life consists in knowing
ourselves more and more, in familiarizing
ourselves with ourselves more deeply, in
becoming increasingly more who we are.*

—ROBERT HARTMAN

Self-leadership is the foundation upon which all other leadership is built. If you cannot lead yourself well, then why would others want to follow you? Everything rises and falls with the leader.

What do you believe is your responsibility for how you show up as a leader? When you accept the role of a leader, you are accepting responsibility for the outcomes of that group; you are not accepting responsibility to personally do that work. Your job is to influence others to get the work done. Leaders influence others through how they show up, and that requires a considerable amount of intention around being self-aware—being clear about the kind of person you are and your ability to self-manage. These are elements of emotional intelligence.

Awareness of who you are, what you stand for, who you want to be, and how you want to show up to others gives you the power to be your best and to make choices that create a healthy work environment for others. Self-awareness also helps you develop the relationships you want and need to be able to create high-performing teams. Leadership requires a commitment to yourself and your own growth and development. It requires self-reflection and strategies for obtaining regular feedback on your behaviors. As you will learn in chapter 4, so much of what you bring into the present moment is hidden, such as your energy, beliefs, assumptions, and emotions. So much operates beneath your conscious awareness. Learning ways to bring more of yourself into consciousness will benefit you in your leadership role. You must become a self-study project!

Through the work we do to increase our awareness of ourselves, we learn how to be more effective, more confident, and less stressed. As we work on ourselves, we can then learn how stress manifests in others, recognize emotions as information, approach people with a trauma-informed lens, and reduce the friction and stress that hold people back from doing their best work and bringing their best to the work and to the world. We start with ourselves.

John Maxwell often shares that people come up to him and declare that they want to be just like him! As one of the highest-paid speakers in the world and one of the most successful experts on leadership, he has led quite an interesting and fantastic life. People want that for themselves. His response to their declaration, however, is simple: "Are you willing to do what I have done?" He did not get where he was overnight, nor did he get there without a tremendous amount of work, perseverance, faith, willingness, study, and mistakes.

Success does not happen without intention and attention, without taking steps and making the effort to move in the trajectory of your goals. Success as a leader requires you to move through your habits of thought, overcome resistance and fear, and be open to new perspectives. Introspection and reflection are not comfortable. They require honesty with yourself and a willingness to be open to feedback, to be vulnerable, to be fallible. As a human, you will make mistakes. How you handle those mistakes as a leader matters. A leadership coach can assist you in exploring yourself, your relationship with failure, your blind spots, and your level of awareness, as well as helping you stay focused on your goals. Often our egos block us from looking within as a form of self-protection, and we require someone else to help us navigate our thinking.

Why This Book? What's This Going to Do for You?

Entering the healthcare field in 1993 sparked my fascination with leadership and set me on a path to study leadership through graduate school and doctoral research, reading hundreds of articles and books and practicing leading in leadership roles. I have been working with leaders as a coach and developing others through mentoring, training, and teaching for three decades. I am on a mission to help you find your power as a leader, reduce your stress, and reduce friction for your team, as well as increase productivity, happiness, and well-being for you and your employees.

My desire to help others in leadership was further fueled when I began working as a director of nursing in 2012. Although I had been a nurse for a long time and had led other initiatives, this would be the biggest role of my career. I would be responsible for 175 adolescents, 40 staff, and six nursing stations over three campuses. When I arrived on the job, I was handed a set of keys and basically told to "have at it." The keys did not even get me into all the places I needed to go! I had to ask for the addresses of two of the sites as no one had provided me with that information. I had no tours of the sites (like, where are the bathrooms?) and no training when I arrived—aside from the human resources training that everyone was responsible for taking. I did receive a list of people that I should probably speak with (directors and other managers), along with a list of my employees and some information on each of them.

Do you think that I was being set up for success?

Unfortunately, this is not all that uncommon. You may have a similar story of your own about how you began a leadership journey, or perhaps you know someone who was treated similarly. Think back to when you first started in your leadership roles. Were you prepared? Were you scared? The responsibility was so great. Did you even understand all that you were responsible for or what authority you had? How did you figure it out? How did you learn how to lead? What did you need to succeed? Did you have support, training, guidance, and mentoring? Or was it more like jumping into the water to see whether you would sink or swim?

About six months after I started this leadership role, the human resources director came into my office and admitted, "We haven't treated you very well, have we?" I can remember that moment vividly.

I was angry. I had been holding in my emotions—emotions I did not even realize I had. Tears started rolling down my face. It was not the reaction I would have hoped for, but I was caught off guard. It felt good to release the hostility and anger and fear I had been holding on to. *Oh my gosh, someone noticed me!* He told me how incredibly resilient I was and that anyone else would have quit already. Then he apologized.

It felt good to be seen, noticed, and acknowledged. I still had to figure it all out myself, and there was so much to fix—so many inefficiencies—but at least now I had support. It seemed that I created an ally that day. I had no intention of quitting; I wanted to do this work, and I felt like I was the right person in the right place at the right time. There was much for me to do and plenty for me to learn.

We learn how to lead by practicing what we have learned about leading through our studies and by watching and experiencing the leadership of others. Being in a position of leadership for a period of time offers you the opportunity to try out your skills and refine them over time. Leadership skills must be developed on the job. I have studied leadership for three decades, but it was when I was in the role of a leader that I learned the most about how leadership really works. And I learned a good bit about myself.

I am passionate about leadership because no one should be sent out to lead on their own without adequate resources and support, regardless of employee level or leadership role. Yes, I am resilient. Yes, I have been through a lot in my life and know how to come out standing strong. And yes, I knew what needed to be done to turn this into a great nursing department. I had studied business and had run my own business for a decade by that time. But I needed support, equipment, and some other essential elements (like keys) in order to perform the job as expected. I am dedicated to ensuring that people have the skills they need to lead and do it well, and I will do my best through these pages to provide you with the tools you need to gain confidence, reduce your stress, find your power, and lead others to higher levels of success and productivity.

We will start by exploring the impact and cost of ineffective leaders. Happy reading!

CHAPTER 2

The Cost of Ineffective Leadership

> *Every adversity, every failure, every*
> *heartache carries with it the seed*
> *of an equal or greater benefit.*
>
> —Napoleon Hill

I did not know what I wanted to do when I grew up, so after several years of college and working odd jobs, I obtained a degree in business. This missed the mark, however, because I loved helping people be their best and feel good about themselves and realized I wanted to be in a position to be of service. So, after graduation, I enrolled in nursing school and accepted my first position in healthcare as a mental health technician (also known as a direct support professional) working in an acute care psychiatric hospital on an adolescent unit. I was excited about the opportunity and the potential direction for my career.

Two major things happened while I was working in this position. The first was that I loved it! I loved working with the kids, and I loved the work. It felt like home. Finally, I felt that I had found a place of belonging after so many years of searching.

This was not easy work. Psychiatric work environments can be dangerous, and they require a lot of self-management. This work is known as emotional labor, which, although rewarding, can be quite exhausting.

The second thing about this job that had a significant impact on my career was that I experienced a really bad and ineffective leader. I'll call her Beatrice (not her real name). Beatrice created an uncomfortable and toxic work environment. Her behavior made our job more difficult and more dangerous. Our unit experienced a high turnover, disgruntled employees, and lots of complaints. No one wanted to work on that unit; the adolescent population is challenging enough without her making it worse.

People lived in fear and walked on eggshells when she was present on the unit. We had to be very careful with what we did or said because she could easily get angry and become reactive—and this could set the patients off if she was on the unit at the time. Beatrice might hold things against you, and people would know she was unhappy with you since she would make a spectacle about it. She could be humiliating and demeaning. She appreciated having power over people and brandished that power whenever and wherever possible.

Communication is such an important part of leadership, and on a healthcare unit, it is especially important that we are all clear about the expectations and that we work together as a cohesive team, as this can impact the patients and our ability to provide quality care. On a behavioral health unit, communication is essential for everyone's safety.

Beatrice created additional uncertainty since we never knew what she was going to do. We had to double-check her instructions with one another and ensure we were all on the same page because her instructions were never clear, and she often told one person one thing and others something else. Since she had her favorite employees, that created a rift between the in-crowd and the out-crowd and caused power differentials between employees. Some people would get away with certain things while others would suffer her wrath for the same or a similar infraction. If she was around when trouble started with patients on the unit, she would bark orders at people. Beatrice was an administrator, not a skilled psychiatric practitioner, which meant she did not always know the right way to proceed. She was also not a doctor, so besides being disrespectful, her requests held no weight. Nurses can only accept orders from a licensed physician.

Since the patients we worked with were at times difficult and could be manipulative and challenging, having to navigate these additional land mines added to the stress we endured. The work itself was hard enough! Her presence and behavior made everything that much harder.

At the time, I was in my twenties, and I knew there had to be a better way to treat people, a better way to lead and to create a work environment where people were happy in their jobs and felt respected and valued. While I would have preferred learning from a healthy leader who could have seen the best in me, encouraged me, and developed my potential, I am grateful for the lessons I learned from that experience. I had to learn how to develop professionalism and integrity despite this administrator. And we all had to learn to collaborate, keep people safe, and trust one another when it counted most.

Adversity and difficult situations force you to learn who you are and what you are made of. This situation helped me develop strength and resilience and fueled my desire to study leadership, to practice leading, and to become an effective leader, and for that I am very grateful. The connection between the leader and that leader's impact on the unit was so obvious to me, and I wanted to learn more about what makes for a good leader. This desire eventually led me to obtain my doctorate in leadership, studying the leader's impact on the work environment and researching the impact of the work environment on employee outcomes.

Sometimes, to learn what makes something good, we must explore what makes something bad.

Ineffective Leadership Styles

We learn a lot from what *not* to do.

Think about the worst boss you have ever had. What was that experience like? What did that leader do that made it bad? How did it feel? How did work get accomplished? What made this person an ineffective leader? How did working with them impact you, your behavior, and your state of mind? What impact did your behavior, thoughts, and feelings then have on other areas of your life and on your relationships?

Aside from the Machiavellian boss who is manipulative, distrusting, and deceitful, there are many attributes of difficult and ineffective bosses. There are bosses who micromanage, take credit for other people's work, and do not provide adequate instruction. Some bosses are absent or laissez-faire, meaning they are present but don't do much to address issues, offer support, or provide guidance. Many bosses simply lack leadership skills and are doing the best they can with the knowledge, information, and support they have available to them. Many of us have not received adequate mentoring and instruction on how to lead well.

Unfortunately, I have had several personal experiences with ineffective leaders. Each taught me things I never wanted to do. Earlier in my career as a nurse, I worked for a short time with an insurance company managing workers' compensation cases. On my first day, the leader gave me a tour of the office, and while showing me around, she pointed out people by some personal quality rather than by name—the blond over there, the guy in the green shirt at that cubicle. Although she did have over 100 employees, which would make remembering names somewhat challenging, she made no effort to learn anyone's name or anything about them. Her behavior seemed to communicate how she felt about her own level of importance and that no one else really mattered. It was very disrespectful. She did not seem to understand just how important each one of those individuals was to the success of the team and the department. It was not lost on me that six months later, the whole workers' compensation case management division was closed, and we were all laid off.

People who gain power through promotion often misuse that power. As Henry Kissinger stated, "Power is the ultimate aphrodisiac." Instead of using the power of their position for the betterment of all, some managers use it to make themselves look good (narcissistic perhaps), achieve a personal agenda, and make a good impression on others. These managers focus on looking good rather than on being good or doing good. They don't care about or empathize with others but rather focus on achieving their own goals.

Power-loving managers make sure you know they have power over you. They can hoard information, not communicating fully or effectively so that people are left questioning the expectations for their work. One of the main areas of frustration at work is a lack of clarity. If your evaluations, bonuses, and pay increases depend on certain standards and expectations but you are not informed as to what those are, how can you succeed? It is unsettling and exhausting. And while people will do the best they can, they cannot achieve goals if they are not explicitly told what those goals should be! Or if the goals are so unrealistic and unreasonable that success is an impossibility.

Power differentials can lead to entitlement. People justify their behavior because of the power they believe they have. An example of this would be when the leaders of an organization take big bonuses, yet their staff do not receive raises, something I experienced for several years while working in healthcare. This behavior reflects a practice of inequality that increases stress and produces bad feelings toward the organization. There is a certain level of respect that comes with a title or position. However, taking advantage of your position or insisting that people treat you a certain way because of that title can be stressful. Instead of power being a useful tool, it becomes a weapon. It shifts the focus of employees from doing good work to pleasing or impressing the boss, which diminishes the team's effectiveness. Pride is a leader's enemy in that the leader then focuses on themselves rather than on those they serve.

Bullies and indecisive or absentee bosses are all ineffective leaders, creating stressful situations and increasing employee dissatisfaction. Additionally, managers often lack the ability to handle conflict and challenging situations. They don't have the skills—and organizations may not have the resources—to provide training or guidance. Silence gives behavior permission, so the ineffective leader who avoids addressing conflict in the workplace ensures it will continue, as they do nothing to stop it and prevent its recurrence. Help in navigating difficult situations, conflict, and even difficult personalities are some of the most common coaching conversations I have with leaders. Dealing with conflict, or sometimes even recognizing that something is a problem, can require a level of acute attention where leaders often lack the skill, support, and comfort level or confidence to address the situation.

There are many ways in which leaders can be ineffective. Some might not delegate effectively, some might not encourage teamwork, and others might not hold people accountable. Ineffective leadership has a cost. The impact on the leaders themselves and on the team is tremendous. If leaders could recognize that impact and make different, more deliberate choices, it would make a big difference in employee well-being and productivity as well as their own.

The Impact of Ineffective Leadership on Oneself

One of my coaching clients, I'll call her Sharon, shared her experience of being in a leadership role. She had been promoted to nurse manager because she was a well-liked and highly skilled nurse, but she received no training in leadership to be able to perform that role. She could not figure out how to make her life manageable as she attempted to deal with the work and the people on her unit. When someone would ask her for assistance with a patient, for example, instead of helping them figure out the next steps, she would literally take over their work. She struggled to get her own work done because she was always busy with her staff's work and the direct patient care. It can be challenging for people to make the leap from individual contributor to manager. She wound up so stressed-out and overworked that she stepped down after only two years. She did not realize the problem until years later and wished she had learned better leadership skills during that time. She might have stayed longer in that management role.

Ineffective leadership practices can impact the leader's reputation, health, relationships, and ability to perform at peak levels. Like my client in the paragraph above, you may find yourself with a bigger workload, staying late to get things done while other people leave on time. You may experience increased levels of stress at work and at home and fear over how you will get it all completed. You may have difficulty sleeping and develop issues with your physical health (e.g., heart problems, high cholesterol, obesity, frequent colds, other physical ailments), mental health (e.g., anxiety, inability to relax, depression), emotional health (e.g., snapping at people, irritability), and even spiritual health (e.g., feeling disconnected and out of touch with your higher purpose).

If you are so busy and put in many hours at work each day, your relationships may suffer. There may not be sufficient time to think, feel, or even just be still. You may have become someone who spends so much time task-hustling that you struggle to relax. One coaching client shared that her husband teased her about her inability to relax. If she had five minutes, she would be looking for something to do to fill that time; otherwise, she said, she felt like she was wasting it. He just wanted to spend more time with her.

This need to do more, have more, keep up, be busy, and be seen as busy—and not lazy—drives us and society encourages it. But when you are moving at 100 miles an hour, you cannot think clearly. Not enough time is spent thinking and reflecting, which is needed to access your creativity and be innovative, strategic, and proactive. You struggle to zoom out to see the bigger picture, which makes it challenging to focus on the future. You become overly focused on what needs to be done right now and may tend to be reactive when anything impedes or interrupts your efforts. There is a false sense of urgency to everything, which can interfere with your ability to connect the dots, synthesize information, strategize, or problem-solve.

For the first few years of my executive role, I fell into this trap of being really busy and working really fast to get it all done. I still wanted a life outside of work, so I worked really fast all day so I could leave at a decent time to be home with my family in the evening. But there was just so much work! I had adopted this notion that it had to be fixed, and it had to be fixed now. I had inherited significant chaos and misspending, and I wanted to clear it up. But that problem had existed for many years before I got there.

The stress was starting to eat at me—literally. I suffered weight gain and two cracked teeth from nighttime teeth grinding! It was costing me. I was using adrenaline and caffeine to get me up and keep me going during the day; then I would crash in the evening. This was not a healthy way to live.

While I thought this was what people expected of me, that was a story I had created in my own mind. No one expected me to work this way. I was doing this to myself. I decided to slow down and spend time reflecting on what was important to me about my leadership and my life, how I wanted to enjoy and experience my role, and what I wanted to create within my department.

It took me years to learn how to operate at a slower pace (I'm still learning!). I was so accustomed to moving fast and getting so much accomplished, but to what end? Why was it important to move so fast? What was the point of that? And how did it look to others? People saw how busy I was. Did I wear that as a badge of honor? How was my behavior interpreted? That may not have been attractive to someone potentially wanting to move into my role and advance into leadership. If I wanted things to be different, then I needed to be different.

The Impact of Ineffective Leadership on Others

Are you aware of how your behavior impacts those around you? Most of us are not as aware as we think we are. While your intentions might be good, without awareness of how your behavior affects others, you may be causing people stress, angst, and discord. What matters most is the impact you have. Your intention to lead well has to include being clear about the impact you want to have on others and then checking in on that through personal observation and regular feedback. Often, we do not see or cannot know the impact we have on others until they tell us. This is why feedback can be so helpful. It provides you with the data and the information you need to make informed decisions about your actions.

Like it or not, your behavior has a direct impact on those around you. For example, if you don't communicate clearly and explicitly, you may find that people are unclear about your expectations. This causes your employees to be uncertain, which increases their fears since they may not know how to please you, how to perform well, or how to produce good work. Fear is not a positive or healthy motivator for getting the best work out of employees. In fact, unclear expectations are a leading cause of people's frustration at work and a main reason people seek new employment. Turnover is costly to an organization, and it can be difficult to replace talented employees.

People hold their leaders to certain standards, expecting them to behave in a certain way. It is a type of bias. They are watching you and they are judging you (like it or not). Depending on their experience with previous bosses, they want to see how you might be different and are hoping for a better experience. Part of your responsibility as a leader is caring about how you show up and how you present yourself to the world. People learn what is expected based on what you do. You teach others how to behave and how to treat you through your actions.

When you are stressed-out, that impacts others. If you are frazzled and disorganized, people learn they cannot come to you for assistance—you do not have the space or ability to provide support. If you don't care about your people, they will be more defensive and harder to motivate. If you do not hold people accountable for things they are responsible for, that sends a message to the people you lead. If you do not do as you said you would do, people learn to distrust you. If you are always busy, people may not feel comfortable sharing things with you. If you are reactive, they will fear speaking with you and may not tell you things you really need to know.

In the story I told about Sharon in the previous section, how might the staff have felt when this nurse manager took over the care of their patient for them? We could guess that perhaps they felt "saved." She may have been known as the rescuer. Sharon never stopped to consider whether that was the role she wanted to play as a leader. Additionally, there was a missed opportunity for professional development and advancing the nursing staff's skills in caring for their patients.

When there are power disparities at work, it can lead people to feel helpless, powerless, fearful, negative, or pessimistic. People shrink to fit into their "place" as opposed to expanding, being free to be themselves, be authentic, speak up, and offer ideas.

If identified problems are managed by finding someone to blame, this can lead to a fearful culture, where people hide issues or problems and fear being exposed, shamed, and embarrassed. In healthcare, it is important that people feel comfortable sharing concerns, issues, or mistakes such as medication errors, for example, so they can be corrected and documented, and future events may be prevented.

When I started as director of nursing, there was a procedure for reporting medication errors, but no one followed it, so I put a new system in place. At first people were scared, especially when I asked them to explain what happened. Eventually, people realized that the focus of inquiry was not blame; they were not in trouble. The goal of having a system to capture medication errors was to support them in not only correcting the error and managing it in the moment— including caring for the patient and ensuring appropriate notifications and documentation—but also to process the event to see how they might do things differently in the future. This would enable them to learn from their mistakes to prevent future occurrences. Tracking errors also enabled us to identify trends and system breakdowns that required us to formulate a different approach. We were all able to learn from that and make the necessary improvements.

People need to be able to speak up without fear of being ridiculed or blamed. No one likes to make mistakes, no one wants to be wrong, and no one wants to get in trouble—yet we will all make mistakes. And mistakes often lead us to learn important lessons. They teach us what we did not know we did not know.

People are impacted by the behavior and energy of their leader, and when the leader behaves in ways that increase stress, fear, uncertainty, or confusion, it negatively impacts people's ability to show up fully to work. This can lead to dissatisfaction, sickness, turnover, poor morale, lower productivity, and disengagement. By changing your approach to work, you lessen the stress you place on others, which enables people to be more productive, creative, and engaged at work, and that has a big impact on the bottom line.

The Cost of Ineffective Leadership to the Organization and Community

Since you go with you wherever you go, your stress from work goes home with you and into the community. The pressure, anxiety, and tension we carry follows us into our activities outside of the workplace. When you are stressed-out, it's hard to be effective at work and hard to be loving and kind at home.

When you are happier and less stressed, that impacts your energy, productivity, and how you show up at work—and in other areas of your life. This impacts those around you and affects how you treat them, so they are less stressed, happier, and more productive. This in turn impacts the organization as you save money in reduced sick time and morale issues as well as increased productivity, retention, and satisfaction. Your organization becomes a more attractive place to work. There is a ripple effect when you work on yourself to become a better leader and a better person.

In 2022 United States Surgeon General Vivek Murthy released the *Surgeon General's Framework for Mental Health & Well-Being in the Workplace*.[13] The report calls attention to what Murthy considers a public health issue. It offers a framework consisting of five essential elements for achieving workplace well-being: protection from harm, connection and community, work–life harmony, mattering at work, and opportunities for growth.

We can no longer afford to consider work as separate from our lives. Work contributes to our lives in significant ways. We need workplaces that support people to be their best and leaders who care about employees and see each person beyond their title or deliverables. We need leaders to provide an atmosphere of safety, respect, and understanding. This requires leaders to approach leading differently. The key for us is to identify how—what would a less-stressed workplace look like? What would it feel like? What would be different? How would people behave? And most importantly, what qualities of leadership would be required?

The price of experiencing ineffective leadership is increased anxiety and stress, fear, silos, lack of confidence or even impostor syndrome, and not feeling valued or validated—and this takes its toll on individuals and organizations. It leads to disengagement, dissatisfaction, and mental and physical health issues, and it impacts our well-being as well as that of those we lead. That impacts the bottom line for your organization, which experiences the costs of turnover, decreased productivity, difficulty hiring, burnout, increased use of sick time, and lack of organizational commitment or loyalty, as well as a lack of innovation and creativity. We have become a stressed-out society, and we need to do something different so we can be our best, thrive at work and in the community, and enjoy a great life at work. We can do better.

Let's explore what effective leadership looks like and how leadership can be done well.

CHAPTER 3

Elements for Leading Well

Leadership is not about a title or a designation.
It's about impact, influence, and inspiration.

—Robin S. Sharma

Think of the best boss you ever had. What were they like? What were some of the characteristics that made them effective? What did they do that made you feel this way about them? What was your experience like working with them? How did working with them impact you, your behavior, and your state of mind? What was the impact that your behavior, thoughts, and feelings then had on other areas of your life and on your relationships?

Consider people of influence, leaders in your community, or public figures you admire. What makes you respect and admire them? What makes you want to follow them? How do they influence people or motivate others to accomplish things?

There are many different leadership styles and approaches to leading. Yet audiences I have worked with over the years all say similar things when describing what makes a leader effective and someone they would want to learn from and follow: clear communicator, good listener, open-minded, fair, empathetic, understanding, believes in me, trustworthy, honest, and possessing integrity.

What makes a leader effective is based on how they show up as a person and what they do to inspire and influence the people they work with. Effective leaders provide clear direction and purpose, offer autonomy and agency, challenge and stretch people to be their best, connect with people, and believe in people. Effective leaders know where they are going, think ahead and plan purposefully, and clearly communicate that vision and their expectations, so people know how to behave and perform. They offer support and encouragement and make people feel competent, confident, capable, and included. They themselves are competent and confident in their abilities, display authenticity and a willingness to be vulnerable and fallible, and address issues that might be steering the group off course.

We know good leadership when we experience it. It feels good. It makes us better people. We feel good working with and for that leader. We want to succeed, and we want that leader to succeed. We become good followers and produce good outcomes. We grow under that person's leadership, and some of us will advance to new positions. There is minimal conflict and turnover, and people are engaged and enjoy coming to work and being part of the team.

Define Leadership for Yourself

It isn't the best leader that people follow.
It's the most followable leader.

—MARK BOWDEN

When you think about leadership, what kind of leader do you want to be? What qualities do you feel are most important as a leader? How do you want to be known as a leader? What does good leadership mean to you?

Great futures are created, and if you want to create something great, begin by envisioning what great leadership looks like for you. This exercise enables you to be intentional about who you want to become as a leader and then, what behaviors you need to adopt to achieve that. Envision yourself as the exceptional leader you want to be. What is that person like? What are the qualities you would like to espouse? What is important to you as a leader? What do you value as a leader? How do you want others to experience you?

When you think about other leaders you admire, consider what they did that you respect and admire, as well as things you might want to do differently. Did they work late at the office or send emails at midnight? Or did they have boundaries around their time yet were still available when needed? Did they have a vibrant life outside of work? Were they rushing all over the place? Organized? Thoughtful and reflective? Proactive or reactive? Did they communicate well? How? In what ways? How did others feel around them? How did they treat others? How did they seem to treat themselves? What made them a great leader?

Some of the words people use to describe how they would like to lead include good communicator, listener, present, empathetic, supportive, available. Effective leaders are trustworthy, have integrity, provide a vision and purpose for the work, and have clear expectations. They are ethical and do the right thing even when it is hard to do so. You know what to expect from a leader like this.

It will be important for you to define great leadership for yourself. What kind of leader do you aspire to be? As we work through the next few chapters, you will be asked to take stock of the kind of leader you are now. That gap between your current state as a leader and your ideal represents your developmental needs and shows you the path to becoming the effective leader you want to be.

In developing your leadership image, consider your personal values—what is important to you. One coaching client mentioned during a session that her leader was never available, so being available and accessible to her staff was important for her, and she admitted this also meant she needed good boundaries. Another client stated that he really wanted his people to succeed, so he spent a lot of time developing others. Another client wanted to work on becoming more effective at addressing conflict, as opposed to avoiding it, as he valued harmony in the workplace.

A high-level leadership client found herself being described by others as "hardworking." We discussed whether that was an important descriptor for her. Was that how she wanted others to view her? Perhaps, given the work she does, this was positive. She admitted, however, that there was an element of wanting to prove herself competent and worthy. She stated that she would like to be effective in other ways by delegating more of her work and developing her staff.

Values guide our behaviors. Yet often, we don't spend a lot of time or effort exploring what we value and what is most important to us. When we are unclear about our values, we miss the opportunity to improve our well-being, decrease our stress, and add value to others. Values unexplored may go unexpressed.

Another consideration for defining your leadership image would be to contemplate how you want others to describe you as a leader. This is known as developing your personal brand. Branding is an intentional strategy for defining your value proposition—the promise of what people can expect of you. It helps you communicate who you are and what you stand for as you present yourself to the world. The impact you have on others evokes an emotional response and produces attitudes in those with whom you interact. It influences basic perceptions that lead to automatic, powerful responses and positive feelings.

Think about someone in your workplace and how you perceive them. Once you have that perception or mental image, you will treat them in a certain way and speak about them in a certain way. It is a form of judgment; however, this is how our brains work to classify information. By taking time to consider how you want to be known, you can be intentional about the person people experience when you greet them.

Decide how you want to be known by coming up with a few adjectives for how you want others to describe you. This is a simple branding technique. By characterizing how you would like to be known, you can start identifying behaviors that are congruent with those characteristics. This gives you power and helps you define yourself as you intentionally and thoughtfully decide how you want others to experience you.

Once you define the characteristics you want to be known for, then you act that way in everything you do in order to bring about the results you want. Everything matters in expressing how you want to show up: how you respond to things, how you carry yourself (your nonverbal behaviors), how you perform, how you communicate, your personal style, your integrity. People will remember their experience with you even if they don't remember exact details. Make every encounter purposeful and intentional.

As others repeatedly encounter you and your intended brand, you begin to become known in that way. Create feedback loops to hear how others feel about you and learn whether your brand is effective. What you don't know will hurt you. Don't be afraid of what people say; welcome their comments and suggestions. It is their perspective, and you can certainly choose not to do anything with the feedback. Just listen. If something does not seem right, you want to know about it as soon as possible so you can correct it. Knowing right away provides you with the opportunity to make corrections to your behavior before it becomes habit. Mistakes handled well make a statement about your humanness and your ability to accept responsibility for your actions. Pretending that mistakes do not happen or refusing to listen to people will not get you the results you seek. Denial and avoidance are two obstacles you cannot afford if you are to be successful in leadership.

In fact, you already have a brand. You are already known for something—for acting in certain ways and for treating people in certain ways. Technically, you do not own your brand. Others create your brand by how they experience you. Your brand is others' perceptions of you; it is not about you so much as how others interpret their experience of you. The founder and CEO of Amazon, Jeff Bezos, has stated that "your brand is what people say about you when you are not in the room."

Discovering what you are already known for can be helpful in adjusting your personal brand. Becoming aware of how others feel about you is part of raising your emotional intelligence. Those who are emotionally intelligent work to be more self-aware and seek to decrease the disparity between how they feel about themselves, how others feel about them, and who they are capable of being. This requires that you know how you impact others. Your current brand may not reflect the qualities you want to be known for. It is, however, your current reality. Be willing to hear the truth from those closest to you and those you trust.

Ask your friends, coworkers, and family members what you mean to them. Why are they friends with you? What do they appreciate about you or about working with you? This is the time to just listen and take notes. You may be surprised at the impact you make on the lives of others. What do people consider your strengths? How would they describe you to others? How do they value you? Get a picture of how you show up in the world.

In speaking with others, you may discover that you are known for different things in your personal life versus your work life. Is this want you want?

To build the trust required to live up to the "promise" of you, you must consistently live your brand. Integrity never takes vacation; meaning, you cannot embody your brand at work and then behave differently in your personal time. Such inconsistency will be perceived as inauthentic and will ultimately undermine your efforts. The message you send through your behaviors must be consistent, clear, concise, and repeated often. People need to be in front of this message repeatedly. A good brand takes time to build. And if you are recreating or rebranding yourself, you will need to be especially vigilant since people know you to be a different way, and they will need time and evidence that you are who you now present yourself to be.

As you receive feedback from others, that information helps you determine whether you are having the impact you desire. For example, if you want people to describe you as available, compassionate, and a good communicator, what would you need to do to ensure you are perceived that way? Your focus would be to identify those qualities and practice them regularly until they become habit or second nature.

Another helpful approach for defining yourself as a leader is to write out a leadership philosophy. How would you describe what leadership means to you and how you will treat others in your role as leader? What is important to you? This philosophy becomes your beacon and guides your leadership behaviors. Incorporating your values and vision for your leadership, it communicates how you intend to lead and what others can expect of you. What's essential here is that once you clarify your philosophy, you must live into it; once you declare it for yourself, you will need to make your philosophy, brand, and vision come to life.

What Is Your Presence Saying?

Who you are speaks so loudly I can't hear what you're saying.

—Ralph Waldo Emerson

Our actions speak louder than our words. Who you are and how you show up speaks volumes. Your energy radiates from you and people feel it. They will assess you based on your energy before you utter a word. They will respond to that energy and how you carry yourself.

How you dress, how you walk, how you talk, the tone of your voice—all of this speaks to how you feel about yourself and the expectations you have for how you want to be treated by others. It oozes from your essence. If you are angry, for example, that emotion shows up in how you carry yourself. This is what I mean when I speak about "how you show up." It is not just what you do that matters but also the energy behind what you do.

People may experience tremendous stress and angst as they attempt to adjust themselves to respond to a leader's energy, mood, or attitude. Having to manage oneself based on the energy of another can be exhausting. Your energy and your presence have a big impact on others.

Your energy matters. As a leader, you set the tone for your department. Your presence impacts others, whether you realize it or not. As a leader, it is important for you to recognize how you impact others—how you show up and what you are carrying into the room—so you can be intentional about your energy and your presence and create the impact on others that you want.

Early in my career as a coach, I would speak at different companies as a way to gain exposure and meet people. During a lunch-and-learn at a local pharmaceutical company, I was speaking on this concept of energy and how we carry ourselves. I asked the group if they knew someone who, when that person entered the room, would completely change the atmosphere; the person was so negative, demanding, and aggressive that their presence alone would have an immediate impact, where people would become quiet and suddenly shift what they were doing to remain safe and out of the line of fire. Immediately, everyone got quiet, and I knew instantly that that person was in the room! I had not noticed it yet when I had asked the group that question. Sure enough, one man looked around the room, and when no one else responded (and they dare not!), he finally said, "No, I don't know what you mean."

I can laugh about this now, but at that moment, I was horrified. My heart dropped to the floor. This man was that negative and aggressive leader! It was not safe for people to share how they really felt. I felt bad that I had put the participants in a position of discomfort. I had not read the audience well enough yet. The rest of the presentation went fine, but that point was lost on that leader. I learned a lot from that experience.

How sad it was that this man was totally oblivious to how his behavior and energy impacted others in such a powerful yet negative way. As leaders, we have an important responsibility for our impact on others. The fact that he was powerful and influential was wonderful, but the way he made people feel was clearly not positive. And he had no idea how he impacted others. Or he did not care. Was he not paying attention? Did no one tell him? Or was he so self-absorbed that he did not empathize or care about what others thought? Did he care more about his power than people?

You are responsible for how you show up and the experience others have in your presence. You are also responsible for your wake and what you arouse or stir up in others. Your energy speaks loudly. People can feel or sense your mood and the emotions you are experiencing. Others have an experience based on who they are, their previous experiences, their worldview, mood, emotional state, etc., combined with how they feel from your tone of voice, your nonverbal behaviors, your emotional energy, and what you bring into the room. People then adjust themselves to match your energy and stay safe. This requires people to accurately receive the energy you are putting out and then behave in ways that will get their needs met without causing a disruption. If you evoke fear in them, then they will shrink or withdraw. This can be quite tiring depending on what energy both of you bring into the conversation. While you cannot control what others bring into the space you share, you can control what you bring into that space, how you come across to others, and the experience you share.

Research has shown that mirror neurons in our brains help us detect the emotions of others and understand their behavior.[14] These special neurons create a direct link between the sender and receiver through emotions, observed actions, and even the sounds of actions, which help us predict what may happen next. With those predictions, we produce similar behavior as well as similar expressions of emotion. We project our own mental states onto others. It is these mirror neurons that help us to empathize as well as become aware of or sense others' emotional states. Turned inward, mirror neurons are responsible for our ability to be introspective and self-aware. Researchers have observed that when you witness someone else experiencing an emotion, mirror neurons activate the same part of the brain involved when you experience the emotion yourself. This is how we understand one another.

In her book *Fierce Conversations*, Susan Scott asserted that our relationships are built by the conversations we have—one conversation at a time.[15] Scott also stated that "all conversations are with myself, and sometimes they involve other people" (p. 83). Our presence and what we bring into our interactions with others creates our relationships. Knowing who you are and being intentional about how you show up and the experience you want others to have in your presence is important to developing your relationships and your leadership style. This is why we begin our leadership journey by leading and understanding ourselves.

Two Important Activities of Leaders: Reduce Friction and Connect

Most leadership activities boil down to two elements: reducing friction and connecting. With thousands of books and articles on leadership and the numerous complaints about what hinders people's ability to do their work and enjoy themselves at work, these two elements are the keys to unlocking the leadership enigma. We will introduce these elements here, and then the rest of the book provides much more detail to help you understand and embrace them on your leadership journey.

Our job as leaders is to enable people to perform their work easily and smoothly, to create a space where people enjoy working, understand what is expected of them, and have enough autonomy and power to perform at their peak. Leaders should provide instruction and clarity around vision, mission, purpose, strategies, and expectations for what people need to do, how people get along, how they communicate, and the outputs expected. Friction is anything that impedes someone's ability to perform their job, slows them down, makes work more difficult, or in any way hampers, delays, or creates obstacles that interfere with their work.

For example, ambiguity is a torment at work. People who do not know what is expected are less productive, less engaged, less satisfied, and more likely to leave that employer. Much research has been done on the topic of role clarity and its importance to engagement and satisfaction at work. Uncertainty increases an individual's threat level and causes people to experience more stress at work. More stress means more friction.

While some stress is healthy for us, like a stretch assignment or a challenging project that provides just enough fear to push us out of our comfort zone, too much stress impedes our creativity and the intelligence center of the brain—the part of the brain that enables us to think broadly and long term. This means that when we suffer from chronic stress, we are unable to access the best of what we have to offer. This is why reducing friction is a crucial element for creating a workplace where people can do their best work.

Effective leaders care about the workload. We know through research (and for many of us, through our own experiences) that as demands rise, we need more control and resources to be able to perform and provide adequate outcomes. It is not the individual that requires more resilience, more hustle, more energy, more output; the system must provide people with what they need to be able to complete the workload and achieve what is being asked of them. Leaders can evaluate the demands and requests made of their employees (and themselves) with the systems and resources people have available to manage those demands—both the personal resources such as level of competence, education, knowledge, ability, resilience, and how much can they handle and the organizational resources such as the right equipment, training, staffing, mentoring, and growth and development.

The aim for reducing friction is to make it easy for people to work with you as the leader, that you clear a path and get out of the way for people to be able to perform at their best. Additionally, the leader is responsible to advocate for and provide the resources, equipment, autonomy, competence, training, and support needed for people to do their work well. Leaders who reduce friction make it easier for people to do their best work and to thrive, which leads to higher engagement and job satisfaction.

The second key responsibility of a leader is to connect with your staff. People want and need to be seen, known, valued, and cared about. No one wants to be invisible. People want to matter. They want to be respected for who they are and what they can offer. This requires the leader to take time with each employee to be curious about them as a person and listen well, so you understand their strengths, ambitions, values, needs, working style, etc. Do not make assumptions; instead ask about their thoughts and challenges. Don't have the answers; be curious about how others would solve their own problems. We will explore this topic much more in Part III.

Leaders start by learning to lead themselves, becoming more self-aware, and that helps as we lean into learning about others and what makes them tick. Combine that with an understanding of the organization and its mission and objectives, and you learn to maximize the efforts of your staff.

A Lesson in People

We're not on our journey to save the world but to save ourselves. But in doing that, we save the world.

—Joseph Campbell

Working in behavioral healthcare, I learned that traumatized individuals display challenging behaviors, often as a way to cope or come to grips with what they have experienced. They don't know how to process their emotional pain, so they lash out either at themselves or others, or they may withdraw behind a wall of silence. They hide the best of themselves as they struggle to figure out how to deal with whatever they have had to endure.

These behaviors reflect what is going on inside of them because of what has happened to them, the meaning they have made about the event, and how they have processed or internalized their experiences—or not. People in that much pain may use drugs or other substances to cope with unpleasant experiences or find other ways to escape their pain—of which there are many. They may shut down and be unable to cope, and that might be what brings them into the psychiatric facility for treatment.

We are all walking wounded to some degree or another. Each of us has had experiences that hurt us or caused us pain. We all experience so much through our lifetimes. What makes one person more capable than another of dealing with their pain? While many people do not end up as drug addicts or needing a psychiatric hospital to work through difficult or traumatic experiences, people in our communities and working in our workplaces may be struggling just the same, and they are doing the best they can.

As leaders, we can care. We can understand that people are carrying pain. We can show concern and offer encouragement, and we can do our own work to heal and work through our own issues. To be a great leader requires us to become great humans. Then we can be good role models and make it less scary for others to do their own work on themselves.

What is important is that each of us does the work required to understand ourselves, show ourselves compassion, and create a life experience that helps us live our best life without becoming stuck and without emotions driving our behaviors in ways that are not healthy or good for us. You are the course of study, and your life is your curriculum. As life's events occur and you experience emotions, resist judging or wishing them away; use them as lessons from which you must learn.

"Hurt People Hurt People" is a song by The Script. It begins with the words: "You take it out on me 'cause you got troubles at home." When we neglect to heal ourselves and lack self-awareness, we tend to project our issues onto others in ways that are not in our best interest and do not represent our best selves. Our bad behaviors may not be intentional; they may be reactive responses based on our past experiences. We project emotions, old wounds, and pain onto others. In other words, our behavior can get ugly!

This becomes a greater problem as we rise in leadership positions. Not only will our bad behaviors impact our relationships, but they also impact the team, our department, and the organization at large. Our behavior produces a ripple effect.

As we come to better understand ourselves, we become more skilled at managing or regulating ourselves so our hurt and pain do not spill out onto others. By focusing inward on how we show up and what we might be carrying, we learn ways to navigate situations gracefully and intentionally. It is important that we do our own work. By gaining a better understanding of ourselves, we can be more empathetic and understanding as we learn how to recognize the pain in others.

Where are the places you have been harmed? What might you be carrying that you are bringing into your work or relationships? Where might you unknowingly be projecting your pain and potentially harming others? Pay attention and notice how others may be experiencing or reacting to you. Those unhealed, unrecognized wounds impact you and your relationships.

Remember the story about Beatrice, the boss who screamed at me, from chapter 2? She is a good example for explaining this concept and understanding how people who are not self-aware might behave. How she ran that unit and her behavior toward us was not about any of us—it had everything to do with whatever she was carrying from her family history and her need to be seen and to have power and control. She had wounds that she had not healed. Often this is the case when people do not recognize how their behavior impacts others. Some don't care to or are scared to do the work, or they don't know where to begin. Beatrice had access to assistance as she worked in behavioral healthcare, but she would have had to admit that she needed some help, and often that is too hard for people to do.

There is no judgment; people will do as they do. We must learn not to take the actions of others personally. We can only do our own work and be a beacon, a model for others to follow, if they are willing and interested in becoming better versions of themselves.

Think Ahead

If you fail to plan, you are planning to fail.

—Benjamin Franklin

It is easy to get trapped in the daily activities and crises of the moment. Often leaders spend so much energy going, doing, and being busy that they have little time to reflect and assess. They value the time spent speaking with a coach because it is the only time they take for themselves to consider what they are doing, the impact they are having, and where they want to go.

As the leader and the captain of the ship, not only do you need to pay attention to what is going on with your crew and equipment, you need to keep your eye on the horizon to be sure the ship is traveling in the right direction and anticipate problems so they can be successfully navigated.

Taking a broader perspective and being forethoughtful and planful are essential elements for being effective. There is great value in looking ahead, looking around, and assessing options. It requires a mindset shift to slow down enough to become strategic, proactive, and organized. It also requires that you delegate any work you can, so you have the time you need to effectively evaluate what's happening, anticipate needs, and prepare for what lies ahead. Doing so will reduce fear, friction, and stress and increase your confidence and feeling of control, which then radiates out toward others.

To be able to see the bigger picture of how things are functioning in their area of responsibility, reflective leaders step back from their daily activities to take a helicopter view. From this different perspective, leaders can assess their department to see how things are flowing and make adjustments. They can recognize themes, notice patterns, and identify challenges. In their work on adaptive leadership theory, Ronald Heifetz and Marty Linsky describe this concept in *Leadership on the Line* as moving from the dance floor to the balcony to watch the dancers and see how they are communicating, flowing, and moving together. This is an elegant metaphor for how leaders can view their staff and assess how people and systems are working together.

In addition to taking this broader view of their own area of responsibility, leaders must look at the organization as a whole as well as the external landscape. We must pay attention to and learn more about the organization's culture, policies, values, and mission-driven activities. What initiatives are important to the executive team or board? What are the priorities of other departments? Externally, look at the economy, trends, technologies, competitors, regulations, and other areas that might impact your company or area of expertise in the near and distant future. You are the expert in your field, so the company relies upon you to see things that others might not be looking for. Your goal is to be able to connect dots and see how things come together, challenges that might be forthcoming, and opportunities for improvement. Then speak up and share your findings along with novel approaches to solve problems or advance opportunities.

Gaining perspective becomes more important as you rise in leadership. As you gain responsibility, you have access to more of the organization and can view larger areas. You can see more of how things are working together to produce the results you are achieving. By learning to take this wider perspective, you are better able to connect the dots, see where things are not working well, and take the necessary steps to make changes and produce better outcomes.

When leaders do not make the effort to reflect and plan but rather stay focused and enmeshed in daily activities, they lose the opportunity to be strategic in their approach, which is a necessary skillset to develop as you rise in leadership levels. If you zoom out, you can look ahead at what might be approaching and plan accordingly. What worries are in the minds of the folks around you or in your industry? What opportunities or threats could be forthcoming? Forethought, by definition, means that you are thinking ahead and planning for what will be needed in the future. When your staff and your leadership trust that you are planful, thoughtful, and organized, this reduces the stress of uncertainty and the fear that comes from worrying about whether the organization will be prepared to handle whatever challenges it faces.

There are numerous examples of how a leader might zoom out to gain perspective. A simple example might be scheduling for the end-of-year holidays, which might start in the fall. Our nursing department would plan for the summer months, when everyone wanted to take their vacations, by bringing on new staff in the winter or spring and training agency staff so they could be prepared to pick up shifts in the summer. We would also plan ahead by using a vacation calendar that everyone could view. This way, all the nurses knew who would be off during a particular week, and they could work their vacation time around what their peers were planning.

Being able to foresee the future, make predictions, and plan ahead are important roles leaders must play to be proactive and strategic in how things are accomplished. Disorganization and lack of planning by a leader induces considerable stress on those dependent upon the structure leaders can provide. It can also impact on other departments. For example, one year our entire maintenance department took vacation in the last week of the summer, leaving the campus school without the means to move offices and classrooms in time for the start of the school year.

Forethought and planning are important for being proactive rather than reactive. There will be times when you must react to events that could not be predicted or planned for in advance. But one of the most stressful things people endure at work is the frantic nature of reactive leaders who treat everything as urgent, as if everything is a crisis. When people are stressed, they cannot think clearly and cannot perform at their peak. Being proactive is necessary to reduce stress. It gives you time to think creatively, garner support from others, communicate intentions, and even practice "what if" scenarios. Reactive or crisis leadership should be saved for dealing with actual crises and not become a way of leading daily activities.

When a disaster occurs, it can be difficult to think of the best response, given the emotional turmoil people could be experiencing. While it is nearly impossible to consider every potential disaster, anticipating the needs of your employees and your leaders will help you to be more effective, especially in times of crisis. Disaster planning is a crucial step to ensure you will have what is needed in an emergency. At the start of the pandemic, for example, organizations that had a pandemic plan were a step ahead in setting up the processes and procedures needed to keep people safe. Shifting to a planful and proactive mindset helps you remain calm in situations that might otherwise produce emotionally charged responses. Anytime you can plan ahead, consider alternatives, and think things through before they occur can save you time and energy.

Many things can be addressed or thought about in advance. If you wait until everything becomes a disaster, you are leading from behind. Get out in front of things by looking ahead, taking a wider view, anticipating what might be needed, and creating a plan. Gain input from stakeholders to ensure applicability. As a leader, learning to be proactive saves time, provides structure, and even offers people safety and trust when they know they can count on you to consider options thoughtfully, make reasonable decisions, and not be frantic and reactive.

During the pandemic, we witnessed leaders on both sides of the spectrum. Some were planful, thoughtful, and communicative, even saying, "Hey, we don't know exactly how to proceed, but we are in this with you and will be open and honest with you about things"—and they were, communicating effectively as more information became available. Even though all of us were overwhelmed and uncertain, people had faith and appreciated this type of honest communication from their leaders.

Other leaders were absent, checked out, and left others to try to figure things out on their own. Some leaders provided a frantic, haphazard, and fear-based approach. Leaders who believed they were supposed to know everything had a tougher time asking for help from people who could have provided information and expertise. It was messy, and these leaders made it messier.

Adversity shows us who we are and what we are made of. It can shine the spotlight on what we do really well and also magnify our weaknesses.

The key is to decide what kind of leader you want to be in good times and in troubling times. How might you use your strengths to be more planful, organized, thoughtful, and proactive in small ways now, so you grow this skill set for when bigger things occur? We can plan ahead by developing skills now that will be needed when crises occur.

What skills might you need to improve so you can develop a proactive leadership approach—organizational skills? Bigger-picture thinking? Perspective exploring? What people or resources might you need to support you in growing these skills and shifting your mindset? How might you clear space and energy to be more thoughtful and planful? In what ways might you need to slow down to be able to reflect, read up on trends, and talk to others about their experiences, their fears and worries, or their forecasts? What might you be missing that you need to know?

Zoom out. Take a helicopter view. Think about how things in your department are working. What is working well? What could be improved? What might you need to address?

Think about the months ahead. What might you need to pay attention to? What might you need to do now to help you prepare for what lies ahead? Forecasting enables you to start having discussions with people you might need to influence in order to make the changes needed in the future. I call this "planting seeds." Having proactive discussions with people today to get them to start thinking about what might be needed later will make it easier when the time comes to make those decisions.

In the next chapter, we will delve deeper into the concept of self-leadership. We will explore the importance of self-awareness, the role of emotional intelligence, and practical strategies for personal growth. By understanding and leading yourself, you will be better equipped to lead others and create a positive, impactful work environment.

CHAPTER 4

Lead Yourself: The Essential Precursor to Great Leadership

> *If you wanna make the world a better place,*
> *take a look at yourself and make a change.*
>
> —MICHAEL JACKSON

C onversations with my coaching clients can be challenging as I ask questions to take the client deeper into their thought processes. Some questions may feel uncomfortable at times. The safe container created by a professional coach for this type of exploration is what makes the vulnerability possible—if the client is willing to access their deeper thoughts. The coaching relationship is what makes this excavation work possible.

Recently, a leadership client admitted, "It's easier to focus on helping others than to look at yourself." This was an insightful statement. It is harder to look inward because we judge ourselves, and we judge ourselves harshly. That can be so unpleasant that we focus on others to keep the focus off ourselves. We might judge them or compare our situation with theirs. It's a trick of the ego that keeps us from facing our truths for fear that we may in fact be so wrong, so unworthy, so inadequate that we don't want to know, so we avoid looking inward.

The self-reflection this client had been doing had compelled her to look at herself in the mirror. She admitted that she was not happy. Spending so much time and effort helping others, meeting others' needs and demands, and putting a lot of pressure on herself to be all things to all people was stressful and had taken its toll. Her actions made her feel drained and absent from her own life. She acknowledged that when she gets home, she has little energy for her family, and she admitted this is not how she wants her life to be.

Advancing in leadership requires that you expand yourself. The only way to do that is to know yourself—to become more self-aware, better able to manage your emotions, and open to exploring new perspectives. This requires self-reflection, time to connect—or reconnect—with yourself, including assessing your values, desires, frustrations, and challenges. The path to happiness and effectiveness is through—there is no skipping over our own foibles and blind spots (awareness gaps). We must face everything, including our fears. The more we connect with, relate to, and respect ourselves, the better we will be able to connect with, relate to, and respect others, which is required if we are to lead well.

We Don't Lead Paper Clips

Leadership is about people—connecting with others, enabling them to be their best, and building relationships. What has been missing from some leadership efforts is the human side of leadership, with too much emphasis on tasks, ideas, productivity, and achievements. Leaders must learn to balance tasks with relationships, doing with being, and things with people.

Robert K. Greenleaf introduced the philosophy of servant leadership in his classic 1970 essay, *The Servant as Leader.* This concept defines the servant-leader as one who wishes to serve and aspires to lead others. Over the years, Dr. Greenleaf and other researchers have worked to define what this means in practice and what behaviors a servant-leader would demonstrate to lead effectively. This would include elements such as empathy, listening, character, stewardship, and commitment to the growth of others.

In one depiction of this concept, the typical pyramid of hierarchy with staff at the lowest levels on the bottom and the CEO/C-suite at the top gets flipped upside down so that the lowest levels of staff—the staff closest to the customer and the largest area of the pyramid—are depicted at the top and the CEO/C-suite is at the bottom. From this vantage point, the goal of the leader is to share power and to support, grow, and develop their people to ensure the best possible outcomes. This depiction supports the servant-leader mentality, where the leader exists to serve others and the organization as a whole. It is a helpful way to maintain humility and remain in service to those you have responsibility for.

One element of servant leadership is to put people first. Several recent books and articles speak to the notion of humane-centered leadership or human-centered leadership. It's as if we have strayed from and lost touch with what leading is all about. After all, we don't lead paper clips. We lead people. We manage tasks, projects, processes, and policies—but we lead people. People require a different approach than how we would complete a task or address procedures or policy changes. We need to learn how to better care for, and care about, the people we serve. The best way to learn how to treat others is by going within and using yourself as the course of study to learn what it means to be human.

By learning to use yourself as a subject of study through your own life experiences—your emotions, moods, thinking processes, habits, and behaviors—you become better at understanding the human condition. From there, it is a short step to becoming curious about others and what they may be experiencing.

Humility and Hubris

Humility is not thinking less of yourself,
it's thinking of yourself less.

—C. S. Lewis

Effective leaders are able to touch their own humanity. They lead from an inner moral compass. Effective leaders learn to balance humility with a level of confidence required to be assertive and self-assured. Knowing what you value and what is important in any given situation provides guidance when challenges arise. When you are clear about who you are and what you stand for, and when you are able to navigate your inner landscape of emotions, thoughts, doubts, and fears, then you are better able to access your best thinking and make decisions that are in the best interest of the greater good and not get lost or distracted by personal agendas.

To do that—to make decisions based on the greater good—one must balance the two opposing concepts of humility and hubris. Also known as polarities, opposing concepts can both have value, but too much of one without enough of the other causes challenges.

It can be difficult to consider what good can come from hubris. Hubris is defined as being overly confident and prideful.[16] It is an inflated sense of self, an overestimation of oneself—a sense of perfection. Too much hubris can show up as conceit or arrogance. It is a form of pride, the ego needing to be in control, garner attention, and be seen as important and better than others. When the ego takes the lead, that person's agenda takes center stage, focusing on their personal needs and emphasizing self-importance at the expense of the greater good.

Arrogance flips this around, where instead of looking at your own perfection, you see other people's imperfections and judge them as inferior.[17] This way of being lacks humanity—there is no room for humanity when one operates with hubris and arrogance. Hubris separates you from other people since no one can measure up. This can be a lonely place to be.

While it is helpful and acceptable, even necessary, to be proud of oneself, being full of pride can be a leader's enemy when the leader focuses on themselves rather than on those they serve. Hubris might show up when leaders take credit for others' work, speak highly about themselves in comparison to others (self-importance, narcissism), need to be right or have the last word, blame others, put others down, are dismissive, devalue other people, or minimize others' contributions. Someone with too much pride or hubris might be defensive, live in denial, be unwilling to listen, and even compromise their integrity, ethics, or values, putting their pride and ego above doing the right thing. They may abuse or hoard their power, wanting and needing to be in control. Too much hubris can indicate poor self-esteem or self-worth and feelings of insecurity.

This is yet another reason to do your own self-reflection and introspection. If you can identify your emotional and personal needs, you can get them met on your own terms outside of your position at work. Neediness can show up in ways that do not reflect our best selves. And hubris, pride, or arrogance point to a need that is unmet. A part of you wants some attention and acknowledgment. Finding ways to meet that need without putting others down and while recognizing your own humanity and that of others enables you to demonstrate some humility and connect with your fellow human beings.

Consider, however, someone who has no hubris or confidence and is too compliant and restrained. That individual may be unlikely to take a stand for a just cause, advocate, make requests, or speak up in meetings. They might be unwilling to share their ideas, hold people accountable, or address conflict when it arises. We need some hubris to get things accomplished and to have influence.

Humility is defined as being modest, meek, submissive, even unpretentious. Someone who is meek will "go along to get along," but they also will resist their passions or immediate reactions and instead act in a controlled and deliberate manner, the very definition of emotional self-management. It is the ability to maintain self-control rather than being controlled by the situation.

Humble leaders, those who possess modesty and demonstrate humility, tend to do well as they lift others up and develop them to serve the organization in bigger ways. They have the self-esteem to be able to put others first and lift others up as they tend to be less self-involved. They tend to take a long-term view and set up succession plans to ensure a legacy that lives on when they leave the organization. Hubris leaders don't tend to think about others or about their legacy when they leave the organization.

Too much humility, however, may show up in someone as timidity. They may look to others for answers, be self-controlled yet not speak up about what they think or feel, and not take a stand on things that require a strong voice. It can show up or appear as an underestimation of oneself. It is possible for the individual with too much humility to give up their power in an attempt to remain humble and reserved.

Hubris and humility live on a continuum. Somewhere in the middle is a balance between the two. We need humility for self-control, openness to hearing other people's ideas, sharing power, and allowing others to take the spotlight and be valued for what they have to say and what they bring to the team. Yet we need hubris to enable us to be confident, speak up, take charge, and lead. We need to be able to keep our egos in check. There is a fluid balance here depending on the context, the needs of the situation, and what is being asked of us at the moment.

In his book *Think Again*, Adam Grant professes the importance of intellectual humility, of being open to exploring your thinking.[18] He declares that you will be wrong—and often are. And it's true—you cannot possibly know it all, and you cannot be right all the time. There can be many different ways to view a situation. A good leader remains humble and open to the possibility that there are other options, other perspectives, and other vantage points that they may not have considered.

Being open to exploring your thinking and entertaining different views, rethinking, looking at things from a new perspective, and reframing will help you keep your hubris in check. Rethinking requires that you explore what worked well in the past but might not be working now and may not work well in the future. This requires you to be willing to question the status quo and let go of any attachments you may have to keeping things as they have been.

In my role as a leadership coach, I help clients look at things from different perspectives by challenging them and discussing other ways of examining a situation. This enables them to see the situation from an expanded viewpoint—they learn to zoom out. It is not always easy to do this yourself, and the coaching relationship is a safe place to question yourself and explore different ways of thinking. What other strategies might you use to keep your humility and hubris balanced?

Front-Page News

When I attended the Fox School of Business at Temple University back in the mid-1980s, before computers were commonplace, before cell phones, and before the internet, the professor encouraged us to consider ourselves on the front page of the *Wall Street Journal* or some other newspaper—the *New York Times*, the *Philadelphia Inquirer*, the *Boston Globe*. I know, I am taking you back to a time when newspapers were where people got their news—that and the television.

It was an interesting reflection and had a significant impact on me as a young adult. If I was to be front-page newsworthy, what would I want people to see about me? Thinking that at any time what you do or say could be captured in an article and plastered all over the front page can make a huge impact on how you choose to behave and present yourself to others.

Today, this concept is even more significant as it is easier than ever to make the news since everyone has a camera in their pocket and we are bombarded with news online. Take a minute to imagine yourself on the news. What would you want people to see? How do you want to be written about or known?

This reflection forces you to consider your integrity, who you are, and how you want to put yourself out there in the world. There have been times over the years when I have seen people I knew from my youth on the front page of a newspaper or in big headlines, in handcuffs, and the story was about their arrest for fraud, embezzlement, or even murder. We see this with celebrities who lose touch with their morals and integrity and get into trouble. How do you want to be known as you navigate through life?

When I first began my coaching business in the early 2000s, my business coach, Ernest Orienté, introduced to me the concept of permanent video. Similar to the front-page news idea, this concept means that from the time you get up in the morning until you go to sleep at night, you are being watched and judged. Please do not shoot the messenger here! This can be unsettling, and yet it is very true, like it or not.

Your kids and spouse or partner are watching you. Your family and friends are watching you. Your neighbors are watching—they want to know what you have, how you look, and how your lawn looks! Then you go to work, and your staff watch you—after all, you are their leader, their role model. Your boss watches you and so do your peers.

Leaders take responsibility for how they show up and for the person they present to the world. They care about themselves, their integrity, their values, and their impact on others as they navigate through their days. What do people see when they see you?

Envision three symmetrical circles coming together and overlapping with each other a bit (Figure 1). The three circles represent how you see yourself, how others see you, and your potential—the person you have the potential to become at your very best—your authentic self. Ultimately, you would like to close the gap between these three elements, bringing those circles closer together, overlapping more and more, becoming your authentic, best self. We are always works in progress—always in process of being and becoming. When we are intentional about who we are being, paying attention to how others perceive us and obtaining feedback so we can adjust and self-correct, that is how we can become more of who we want to become and bring more of our best selves out into the world.

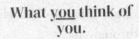

What you think of you.

What others think of you.

What is possible for you to become — your potential or desired self.

Figure 1. Venn Diagram—Self-Other-Potential.

An executive coaching client recently shared that in a previous role she would literally run down the hallway from one meeting to another. A colleague mentioned something to her about how that appeared to others, but at that time in her life, she was proud of being busy and excited to be involved in so many things. It made her feel important and needed, even if it did cause her a lot of stress. Although she is able to laugh at herself today, at that time, she was unable to hear the feedback she was being given.

Leaders have followers, people who want to emulate them. Consider chapter 2 where we discussed bad bosses and their impact. We learn what not to do based on their behavior. Effective leaders adopt behaviors that enable them to become someone others would want to emulate. They accept responsibility for how they show up to others and interact with them, and they model the behaviors they wish to see in others. The impression and the impact they make is positive and hopeful.

Effective leaders have followers, not just titles. Would you follow you? Become the kind of leader that people want to follow. Become the kind of leader you would be proud to have plastered on the front page of the newspaper, or the internet, or your favorite news channel.

The Iceberg: Look Beneath the Waterline

What you are aware of you are in control of;
what you are not aware of is in control of you.

—ANTHONY DE MELLO

Think of an iceberg sticking out of deep waters. The part above the water, what you can see, can be likened to your skills, behaviors, accomplishments, and results—what you do, what you say, how you look, and what you create. This might include your language, customs, traditions, musical tastes, interests, manner of dress, and work. The part of the iceberg above the waterline is everything that is visible about who you are and the life you have created.

Beneath the waterline is everything that cannot be seen, much of which may be unknown to you. This includes things like your deeply held beliefs, how you think, your perceptions, perspectives, worldview, emotions, attitudes, habits of thought, values, biases, assumptions, styles, roles, notions, norms, and desires. Mostly unconscious, these thoughts drive you to behave in ways that create your life experience. Your results, what is visible above the waterline, are your measuring stick for what lies beneath it. These notions, ideas, beliefs, and values were formed long ago along your life journey and perhaps helped you survive. Today, however, these drivers might not be serving you.

Much of what I do as a leadership coach is help clients uncover and unpack what lies beneath the waterline. Asking provocative questions and challenging them without judgment or opinion—just inquiring—helps clients reveal their own thinking and intentions, the purpose behind some of their behaviors, and the awareness gaps or mental models that drive them in ways that are not necessarily productive in their lives today.

To create a great life and to become a great leader, we must become more self-aware and awaken to these hidden habits of thoughts, assumptions, biases, beliefs, and other drivers so that we can become empowered to make changes and choose better actions. We do this by noticing and being curious—paying attention to ourselves—our thoughts, beliefs, emotions, and behaviors. We notice and then name what is going on for us. Be present to yourself, be open to exploration, and be willing to reflect upon yourself and ask yourself some tough questions about why you do the things you do and why you think as you do. This self-reflective practice will help you uncover what lies beneath your conscious awareness.

Self-reflection can be uncomfortable. Coaching is uncomfortable at times because it forces you to think about things you may not have considered before. Coaching done well is going to be uncomfortable, which is why there are professionals who are trained in the process. Friends are comfortable. Family is comfortable. To really change people's lives requires a bit of a stretch, and that can feel uncomfortable.

Learn about yourself. Be curious. YOU are the focus of study—your life is the curriculum. And your homework is to study you—how you think, what excites you, what lights you up, what brings you joy, your strengths, and your weaknesses. Take assessments. Take some time to reflect and perhaps start keeping a journal. Look for ways in which you get in your own way or hold yourself back.

Pay attention to how others see and experience you. When people offer you feedback—compliments or constructive comments—inquire for more information. All feedback is good! Feedback is another person's opinion of you and your behavior. It is their perspective so it's not really about you; it's about them and how your presence impacted them. Ask for specific feedback to learn how others perceive you. This gives you information you can use to adjust your presence and how you show up in the world. Pleasant or unpleasant, feedback is a gift. Unpack it by asking them to tell you more about the impact you had on them. Then just listen and say, "Thank you." We often cannot know the impact we have on others unless they tell us.

Others can also be mirrors for you—what you have distaste for or get annoyed about (or jealous of) or even really like in someone else reflects something in you. Pay attention. Do not make this about judging the other person. Focus on what is coming up for you in that experience of that person. What bothers you and why? Reflect on that.

So often people look at others to compare them with themselves; we can judge others (harshly!) and judge ourselves (harshly!). But there is no one else like you. No one else has the iceberg you have with everything that makes up you, which includes your experiences, education, resilience, and personality. You are amazing! Your job is to find out just how amazing you are and be great. As you learn more about yourself, you become more respectful and loving toward yourself; this enables you to be more respectful and loving toward others.

How you treat others is often a reflection of how you feel about yourself (aside from narcissists who focus all their attention on themselves and care little for others, and at the other end of the spectrum, people who have lost all sense of self, who tend to forget to care about themselves and give everything they have to others). If you are judgmental, critical, and disrespectful toward yourself, then this is how you will treat others. No one who loves and respects themselves will treat others disrespectfully because they would, in effect, be disrespecting themselves. The more you care about yourself, love yourself, accept yourself, and honor yourself—the better you treat yourself—the better you will care for and respect others.

Additionally, what lies beneath the waterline includes the impact from traumatic events you may have experienced. It is essential that you work through any trauma or unhealed wounds as best you can so that whatever hurt or pain lives within you can be tended to and integrated. Your problems and adversities are fertile ground for you to explore, learn from, and grow from. Everything you have experienced has helped create the person you are today. Adversity helps you discover what you are made of. If you feel you need a professional to assist you in this, find a therapist in your area that specializes in trauma work.

Do the Right Thing

Integrity does not take a vacation.

In nursing school, we were instructed on ethics, culturally competent care, compassion for the individual, caring for people with different diagnoses, effective communication, and patient rights. We learned the basics of providing care for people from all social classes in their most vulnerable moments. Then, once we graduated, passed our boards, and started working in the field, we practiced what we had learned and applied it in the workplace.

These first few months are extremely important because it is during this early stage in your career that you establish the habits that will become the foundation for how you perform your work and lay the groundwork for the rest of your career. Most mistakes in nursing can be traced back to someone missing a basic step in the process. The basics are incredibly important, and everything else builds upon performing those correctly.

The same is true for most professions and jobs. You learn the basic competencies and then have to come up with your own way of implementing them to achieve positive outcomes. Those actions then become habits and you perform them automatically, which frees you to focus your attention on other things.

During this elemental time in your career, there is a decision you make regarding your ethical standards and integrity. What are the moral guideposts you will follow? When someone asks you to cut corners, do something unethical or fraudulent, falsify something, or support some other questionable activity, what will you do? This line of questioning asks you to consider the kind of person you are and what you value regarding doing the right thing.

The right thing may not be popular, easy, or comfortable. It requires courage; you will need to speak up in some way. It is important to know who you are regarding doing what is right and what you stand for. Standing up for what you believe is the right thing, the ethical thing, even the legal thing requires what is known as moral courage. You need to know so that your standards guide you when you are faced with challenging situations. And make no mistake, your ethics and moral code will be tested.

As you grow in leadership, there are more things to consider, and the stakes can become higher as well. If you revisit the basics, consider what is important to you. What defines your moral compass? Many professions, including every medical profession as well as coaching, have a code of ethics. When you are faced with a conflict of interest, which no one may even know about without you saying something, what will you do?

On several occasions throughout my career, my ethical standards have been tested as I faced different ethical dilemmas and even ethical disagreements. I was always clear about who I was and what I would do. My license was important to me. We were taught as nurses that although we follow orders written by physicians (or other advanced medical practitioners), we could still be held liable and culpable if we followed an illegal, negligent, or otherwise harmful order. In other words, we were responsible for our actions in relation to the orders we received. I never wanted to be "front-page news" on the wrong side of what was right. Doing the right thing became a sort of mantra for me, and I carried that with me into my leadership role. It was more important for me to be respected than to be liked. People knew what to expect when I showed up on the unit or when I was leading the department. We were always going to remain in integrity and do the right thing—whatever that might be. We may need to figure that out together, but we would always do what was right.

Integrity is that line between what feels right and what feels bad. You know you are out of integrity when you do things that go against your belief system. For example, perhaps you say you want to develop your staff but struggle to delegate. That is a great place for exploration because you could be out of integrity there. Perhaps you say you value your family but then remain at work late and spend time in the evenings and weekends on your laptop or cell phone. That is another questionable area for exploration as your actions are incongruent with your stated beliefs.

Whatever choices you make in your life, they are yours to make. This is where your power lies. Take responsibility for the choice and for the consequences of that choice. This is integrity. After all, you have to live with yourself and with those choices. If one of them turns out bad, you will learn lessons from it. At least you will live by your own standards. If instead you base your decisions on what other people do, what other people tell you to do, or what is easy and comfortable, you give away your power, and you still must live with the consequences.

When you carry yourself a certain way and live up to your standards, then people are clear about what to expect from you. When you see something, say something or do something to correct it. Doing the right thing requires that you discuss what the situation needs and then muster the courage to act, despite what others around you are doing. Following the rules and living in integrity is respectful for you and for those around you. When you uphold high standards, others follow your lead and together we raise the standards. As the saying goes, "A rising tide raises all ships." Sometimes it takes a strong leader to forge the path to higher ethical conduct. Even if you are not at the top of the hierarchy, you can lead from wherever you are. Who will you be? What will you stand for?

What Respectful Leaders Do Well

When we reflect on our lives, we must explore the good and what is going well, not only what you would like to change. Take a few moments to consider what is going well in your life. What do you love about your life? What do you appreciate about what you have created in your life? What are you proud of (besides your kids!)? What are you grateful for?

What do you really like about yourself? (Don't worry, I won't tell anyone!) This is not about ego. The ego comes into play when you compare yourself with others, as we discussed in the section about hubris. We are not looking to compare you with anyone else, only to consider things about yourself that you really like and appreciate—things that are good, things you achieved and overcame in your life, things you enjoy and appreciate about yourself, your special sauce, your uniqueness and quirkiness, things that make you unapologetically you.

What brings you joy and fulfillment? What makes you feel alive? What makes you smile? What values are essential to you, without which life would not be worth living? This is what you want to define your life by and craft it around.

Strengths Finder by Gallup is an online strengths-based assessment tool.[19] If you have never taken the strengths assessment, you might want to check it out. Identifying your top five strengths enables you to be more aware of what makes you come alive; using those strengths every day in some way will help you become more fulfilled and satisfied. We get much more enjoyment from activities when we play to our strengths as opposed to working through our weaknesses and trying hard to be something we are not.

If you live each day in a way that brings you joy, you will live it well. Each of those days adds up to a life you are proud of and glad to have lived. At the end of each day, you can say you lived it well; then at the end of your life, on your last day, you can say you lived a good life.

Why does this matter in a book on leadership? It matters because this is the root of what life is all about—living to the fullest must include enjoying the journey. In fact, having joy in our lives is a protective factor against the challenges and stressors we face. Too often we get wrapped up in what we have in front of us. We stay so busy that we don't take the time to inquire of ourselves and reflect upon what we believe defines a great life, or we wait too long and much of our life has already passed us by. What is a well-lived life for you? How will you know you are living it well? When you get to the end of your life, what would you like to be able to say about the life you've lived, the things you've done, and the impact you've made? What role does leadership play in the impact you want to have in the world?

When we read stories from those who are dying, they share that their biggest regrets are not taking more risks in life, not loving enough, not forgiving sooner. Life goes by so fast. Making the effort to be more awake to life each day is called mindfulness, and being more aware of how you show up and the impact you make, being more intentional about who you want to be and how you want to navigate through life, will ensure you are fully present now, so you don't miss out on the joy life has to offer. Joy can only be experienced in this moment.

If our goal is to move away from the stress of our current way of working, then we must envision a better future. What do you want? What would leadership well-being be like, look like, and feel like? If you could wave a magic wand and have well-being in workplaces today all around the world, what would be different? As Stephen Covey taught us in his bestselling book *The 7 Habits of Highly Effective People*, start with the end in mind.[20]

In the next two chapters, we will work on identifying stressors in the hope that you can find ways to decrease stress for yourself and for those you work with. As we clear space and decrease our stress, we can add things that we do well, that bring joy and peace, and that increase our well-being. We free ourselves to envision a different way of working, playing, living. And we take steps to create that new reality.

In chapter 5 we start to unpack how your thinking creates your reality, and your stinking thinking creates your stress. Identifying the "mind muck" and the ways in which you give yourself a hard time offers you the opportunity to choose a different path. Awareness is the key to unlocking a new way of approaching leadership and finding the power to do something different.

PART II

Minimize Stress to Drive Success

> *A leader is best when people barely know*
> *he exists. When his work is done, his aim*
> *fulfilled, they will say: we did it ourselves.*
>
> —Lao Tzu

I n Part I, we explored how leaders are made, from stepping up into leadership to the ineffective and often haphazard ways we learn to lead. Our experiences with bad bosses and good bosses play a role in the development of our leadership style. We started to look inward to explore ourselves and define what effective leadership means to each of us. Lastly, the two major activities for effective leadership were introduced: reducing friction and connecting.

In Part II, we shift our attention to the first major activity of a leader: reducing friction. We start by identifying our stressors and finding ways to reduce those things that slow us down, create tension, and hold us back. This provides us with the space needed to be able to choose more effective and efficient actions. We will explore how to advance your leadership through self-exploration and identify strategies to reduce your stress, reduce friction for your team, and create a work environment that supports people's well-being at work.

CHAPTER 5

Reduce Friction

> *Only dead people have no stress, never have uncomfortable feelings . . . discomfort is part of life and tough emotions are our contract with life. We don't get to have a meaningful career, raise a family, leave the world a better place, or make our way through a pandemic without stress and discomfort. Discomfort is the price of admission to a meaningful life.*
>
> —SUSAN DAVID

L ife is not meant to be easy, although we wish it was. Watch any show on wild animals or plants and you will witness how they struggle and fight to survive. The environments they live in can be brutal, and they must learn how to conquer difficulties, overcome misfortune and hardships, and keep moving forward. So it is with us humans.

You will face many challenges and overcome many adversities along your journey. Stepping up in leadership offers you opportunities to experiment with yourself and defy possibilities. Along the way, you improve at facing your fears, accessing your courage, overcoming obstacles, and revealing more of your ability and potential.

Stress plays a complex role in our lives. Some stress is good; it enables us to stretch out of our comfort zones and achieve new accomplishments. Any time we are asked to take on a new challenge or reach a new goal, we might feel stress, pressure, anxiety, or fear. This is normal. And it lets us know that we are pushing ourselves to a new level of success, branching out from the known to the unknown to experiment and learn what more we are capable of achieving.

Stress is an inside job. It is what happens when we are faced with new challenges. It is not the challenge itself that produces stress but rather our reaction to the challenge that causes us to feel some kind of way about it. Different requests and situations may result in different emotional states, depending on the context and how prepared we feel for the challenge. That does not mean it is good, bad, right, or wrong. It's just a thing. And yet, because it is happening within us, we can determine how we want to manage the stressful experience. That is powerful. You can choose how you want to feel, how you will approach the situation, and how you will work through it, as well as what resources you might need to succeed.

Resilience is a person's ability to navigate through the stressors they face in life. This includes how you handle difficult emotions, how you think through problems and make decisions, and how resourceful you are to find supports—people and tools—to help you along the way (as well as finding the courage to ask for the support or guidance you need). When we face too many challenges at once, we can reach a point where we feel overwhelmed. This is the stress that requires attention. Finding ways to live our lives where we do not fall prey to overwhelm means constantly assessing our outer world—the things that are coming at us—and our inner world, the ways in which we think about ourselves and the situations in our lives.

Emotions are messages from your inner world, and the data they provide tells you something about the current state of your body, mind, and spirit. Learning to read these inner messages helps you make decisions to aid in navigating both your inner and outer worlds. For example, the message of overwhelm is a need to simplify. You are doing too much and have too little time.

We are in a constant state of being and becoming, and we want to explore both these states in this chapter. How you think, what you believe, and your assumptions and habits can cause you more stress than is necessary. When we add stressors to our lives that are not necessary, it makes life harder and slows us down. It's not helpful, and in fact, it hurts us. These added personal stressors, these ways of thinking and behaving, will be challenged in this chapter. As we explore how you might be adding to your stress and getting in your own way, you will learn ways to let go and consider different perspectives, which will help you move forward in a better, more effective direction.

People often look outside themselves for their answers, perhaps by comparing themselves with others or seeking others' opinions about how to be or how to proceed. Dr. Robert Kegan, author of *The Immunity to Change,* refers to this as the "socialized mind," where we seek validation through the expectations of others, adhering to the definition of ourselves that was shaped long ago as well as what others want us to be and expect of us, as opposed to a "self-authoring" mind where we develop an effective internal compass to guide our choices.[21]

No one can tell you how to best be you. You cannot find what you are looking for in the minds and hearts of others; you must look within yourself to develop your own moral compass, set expectations, and adhere to your own set of values to guide your decisions. Your mission, should you choose to accept it, is to turn inward and explore your inner world—beneath the waterline—so you can become more of what is possible for you to become, better manage your time and energy, and feel grounded so you can be more authentically you. When we give ourselves a hard time, it only serves to hold us back. We need to get curious so we can explore our inner world, our inner operating system.

The good news is that because your inner world is all in your head, you can access it and to upgrade your thoughts and beliefs and question your assumptions. By unpacking the ways you get in your own way, you will tap into your personal power, your power to choose different thoughts and different actions. In this way, you enable yourself to produce different outcomes. By acknowledging and reducing these personal stressors, you develop more confidence and poise in how you present yourself and how you lead others. You expand yourself and open yourself up to new opportunities. You also learn to give yourself much more grace.

Respect Your Mind and Its Beautiful Messiness

*Ever notice that in the long run those who don't
eventually go "within," often go "without"?*

—MIKE DOOLEY

There are many ways in which we give ourselves a hard time and make things harder than they need to be. We don't realize we are doing this, of course. We would not intentionally make life harder than it needs to be. We do our best to navigate our world, and in doing so, we put a lot of pressure on ourselves to be right, to be liked, and to do great work. The thinking in our inner world fuels our behaviors. The good news is that because this goes on in our heads, we can change what we are doing if it is ineffective and does not bring us the results we seek. The difficulty lies in that because it is in our heads, we often have trouble accessing the thinking that keeps us stuck in challenging situations (and keeps us repeating them).

Many years ago, I conducted several keynotes on "The Top 5 Ways to Be Ineffective & Unproductive—and What to Do Instead." During these presentations, I shared different situations, offered the internal dialogue that might be going on inside our heads and the behaviors we might adopt as a result, gave that a name (e.g., people-pleasing, avoiding and escaping, lack of self-awareness, needing to be right, settling for mediocrity), shared why it was unproductive along with the impact on our lives, and then offered a coaching tip. These were fun sessions because the audience could easily see themselves in the situations and could relate to the dialogue that was going on in their heads. We really do get in our way in so many fascinating ways!

The problem is that this is hard to see when we are in the midst of it. We must be able to zoom out to view the situation from a different perspective, pay attention to our thoughts, notice our feelings, and then use both—our thoughts and our feelings—as information to guide us in making decisions. First, however, we need to set some intentions.

Change does not happen without effort. If we want to reduce our personal stressors—the stress we place on ourselves because of how we think and behave—we must first identify what we want and envision life differently. Setting an intention to be more effective, less stressed, and more confident requires that we commit to this process of paying attention to our thoughts and feelings, reflecting on them, and making choices based on what we want to create for ourselves— that vision for our success, for good leadership, and for a well-lived life.

Habits, beliefs, assumptions, biases, culture, worldview, values— these all reside under the waterline. Humans operate out of habit. The mind creates habits so it can be more efficient. We don't have to think about how to drive a car, for example, once we learn how and practice; we only need to focus on the road and other drivers.

Your mind collects information and connects dots to produce conclusions. We make assumptions and draw conclusions based on the information we have gathered. Sometimes we have very little information about a topic. This means that our conclusions are not truth; they are the way our minds have connected the information that was available and made sense of it. The mind does the best it can to synthesize information, given the data it has collected and received over time, which means our assumptions or conclusions are a possibility and not necessarily correct. This is why it's important to not be so attached to being right and why we are encouraged to learn, study, read, and question what we have learned. What we know and how we think may very well be wrong, and information changes over time. We need to be willing to regularly reflect on our thinking and question ourselves and our perspectives.

We Are Master Storytellers

Our identity is the sum of the
stories we tell ourselves.

—TONY SCHWARTZ

"Don't believe what your client tells you." A mentor coach expressed this during a training on the core coaching competency of "listening to the client." What she meant was that our coaching clients tell us stories about their situation. These stories are made up; they are the narratives that clients tell themselves, believe, and live by. If we, as coaches, get caught up in the story, we are not coaching. We have to dive beneath the story to learn more about what the individual was thinking and feeling about the situation. What meaning does this story have for them? What is important about this story, and why did they bring it up today?

Professional coaches help people explore the stories they tell themselves. Humans are master storytellers. We make up stories in our heads about ourselves, others, and the world, and then we ascribe meaning to them. What are you telling yourself about that situation, person, or thing? It's all made up; it's how we describe the situation from our perspective—it's not real, but we certainly think it's real. The more attached you are to your stories, the more stressed you may become when they are challenged. The brain cannot distinguish between real and perceived threats. So, you could become quite stressed from your perspective of the story.

This is all going on in our heads. We must verify (our assumptions) by asking questions of our thinking. Our brains connect dots and try to make sense of things. This is good. It is helpful. Yet we must not get attached to our stories. We could have it wrong, and often do. We could be, and often are, missing data that would help us create a more comprehensive story.

Often, we cannot unpack the story for ourselves—that is where coaching can be very helpful, especially as you rise in an organization. Where else can you go to examine your thinking without judgment?

In working with addicted individuals over the years, we would remind patients not to go "upstairs without adult supervision." This means that one would need to be careful about being in their head and listening to their own thoughts because those thoughts and stories were not to be trusted. I always loved this phrase! If we don't verify the information we have in our heads, we can get ourselves into a quandary and magnify a problem exponentially when we have not yet even verified its existence.

Let me give you an example. Consider this: your boss walks by and ignores you. What stories are you telling yourself? That they do not like you or are mad at you, that they don't have time for you or don't value you? We can make up all kinds of stories. We catastrophize. We blame and rationalize. The inner voice of doubt starts shouting that you are not worthy or worthwhile. Before you know it, you are telling yourself how unappreciated and undervalued you are, and you are ready to quit your job and go work at a local coffee shop!

When you finally come down from your emotional escapade, you realize that the boss just got out of a big board meeting. Maybe, just maybe, they had some other things on their mind and did not pay attention as they walked down the hall. Imagine that—it had absolutely nothing to do with you!

Many people struggle with catastrophizing, where they make up a story in their heads about something, and that story evokes a lot of emotion for them. The story becomes truth, although it is just a story. One way to minimize or lessen the anxiety is to learn to detach from the story, to recognize that it is, in fact, just your mind's way of connecting dots, and then to verify and ask questions to gain more information so that you can better understand the situation and not just be in your own head with that story. In this example, asking your boss if they are OK would be one way of obtaining clarifying information and connecting human-to-human, showing your care and concern for them.

Leading at the Speed of People

One of the first lessons I learned working in a psychiatric facility was not to take things personally. Patients would say all sorts of things and could be quite disrespectful. I learned very quickly that nothing they did or said was about me. Usually it was transference, which is a term that describes how people can transfer or redirect their emotions that were originally felt somewhere else onto another person. Difficult as it may be to detach and separate oneself from what the other person did or said, it was important to understand that the patient was taking their pain out on whomever was there. It had nothing to do with me but everything to do with the emotions or wounds the person was carrying.

Not taking anything personally is important for staying grounded and holding on to your personal power. In his book *The Four Agreements*, author Don Miguel Ruiz shared that when we take things personally (which violates the second of the four agreements), we assume everything is about "me."[22] Me, me, me. Me, myself, and I. This is the (ego's) trap of "personal importance," making everything about you personally when it is not about you at all—it is about the other person.

Learn to ask people what is going on for them instead of taking the story you have made up in your mind as truth (e.g., the boss does not like me, appreciate me, or value me because they did not acknowledge me in the hallway). This is an important lesson in leadership. When you notice something irritating you, step back, detach, and get curious; ask a question of the person to learn more about what might be happening to them.

Respect Yourself

Until you make the unconscious conscious, it will direct your life and you will call it fate.

—CARL G. JUNG

The ways in which you have learned to connect data points (information), how you interpret your experiences, how you learned to perform and behave in the world, how you learned to survive, and what you feel is important—all of this resides under the waterline and may be hidden from you. What is important in your life now might not have been important when you adopted a particular belief or habit. You are different today, and some of your beliefs may no longer be serving you. Unpacking the beliefs and the thinking behind what you do can help you explore what drives you to behave as you do. Recognizing and identifying that something is not working for you enables you to adopt new beliefs and new mindsets that better serve you in your life today.

There are ways you have learned to be in the world that may be blind spots (awareness gaps) for you and may be causing you stress, not producing positive results, and even hurting you, your health, your family, your team, your organization, or the bottom line. Assessments can help you uncover your strengths and areas for development, including 360 assessments where you receive feedback from colleagues, direct reports, and supervisors, which may help expose gaps in your understanding of how you show up and the impact you have on others.

The emotional intelligence assessment I offer my coaching clients, called the WE Intelligence Profile (WE-I Profile), reveals how you experience relationships when triggered or activated in difficult interpersonal situations. *"WE Intelligence reflects our ability to be present with our experience and that of others during stressful encounters and do so without protecting or defending ourselves or initiating some form of coping to distance ourself from the distress of it."*[23] This behaviorally based assessment (as opposed to a self-report) is offered through the Learning in Action® company and exposes your internal response in the moment when under stress in your relationships. It explores your tendencies to access certain emotions under stress, how you tend to self-regulate, and your access to empathy when you are under stress. Visit my website to learn more about this helpful tool if it interests you.[24]

One of the areas captured by this assessment is the concept of orientation, which reflects how you view others versus yourself and the responsibility you accept in navigating relationships. For instance, some people take on way too much responsibility for relationships. Assuming responsibility beyond what is within your control can cause stress, and you may worry that perhaps you are not doing enough (to remain in the relationship). In this way, you give up your power and allow the other person to avoid taking responsibility for their part in the relationship (or project).

A leader who takes on too much responsibility may have difficulty delegating and sharing the work. They may have difficulty staying in their lane and take on too many other tasks, get involved in too many projects, and even struggle to prioritize.

Other folks can be so focused on others that they have lost touch with themselves and their inner world. They may blame others for things not being as they expect or want them to be. They may have difficulty accessing their own emotions or be unaware of their role in the situation. They may have trouble seeing or owning their contribution to things—good or bad. In so doing, they, too, give up their power and need to learn how to explore their inner world. When a person is so focused on others, they have lost touch with themselves and often have difficulty accessing their feelings. They just know that others are not doing what they should. The focus is always on what others could or should be doing and not on how they themselves might be contributing.

It can feel bad to be on the receiving end of this type of leadership. It may feel like you can do nothing right. It might be that you do not have clear instructions or expectations and therefore have difficulty producing effective work. This leader might have difficulty sharing positive (or even appropriate constructive) feedback or offering praise for a job well done.

I tend to be the first type and take on more responsibility than is mine to accept. I had to learn to stay in my lane and let go of the rest, even though I could see what needed to be accomplished and even though, perhaps, things did not get completed in a timely manner. It did not serve me to take on all the work. It only made me more stressed, overwhelmed, and frustrated. I had to allow others to work at their own pace and do what was theirs to manage.

This is one of many ways we can make life harder than it needs to be. We must find ways to expose these areas of stress and frustration so that we can be more effective leaders. The ways in which we get in our own way include things such as limiting beliefs, old and outdated perspectives, faulty assumptions and conclusions, and biases. These habits of thought are running your life and may not be serving you. It is not easy to uncover these thoughts and beliefs and excavating this "mind muck" requires time and attention. You may find that a coach can help you uncover these subconscious patterns and blind spots. After all, we call them blind spots for a reason.

Create a process to self-reflect, perhaps by using a journal, and notice your thoughts and the stories you tell yourself, any discomfort you may be feeling, and behaviors you seem to engage in regularly that might not be bringing you the results you seek. This requires a good bit of self-exploration to become more self-aware because there are forces at work to keep you as you are.

We become numb to the pain in our lives. The brain turns off what it gets tired of. The brain also moves us from discomfort to comfort, meaning that eventually, we become accustomed to discomfort as it becomes familiar. Additionally, change can be uncomfortable, so the brain works to keep things the same. The brain likes harmony and the status quo—there are no surprises there. The brain knows you will get X result if you follow this well-trodden path. Yet you won't know what needs to be edited, updated, or changed without exploring and examining your habits of thought. This means we must become present—to wake ourselves up—and face the fear and the pain of whatever is bothering us.

The goal is to uncover what is not working, identify how you are getting in your own way and holding yourself back, and then clear the path so you can achieve better results. Reducing stress and friction in your own life can help you then clear a path for those who report to you. The first step is to notice and be curious about what drives you to behave or think in a certain way.

Take a Deep Dive into Your Pain Points

The best and easiest place to start is with your frustrations. What are you putting up with? What drains you right now in your life? What keeps you up at night?

If something or someone is not adding value to you, then it is depleting you in some way. This means you have less energy to do the things that really matter to you. Where do you spend your energy?

While most people think about and concern themselves with time management and doing more, the authors of the book *The Way We're Working Isn't Working* argue that it is your energy that matters, rather than your time.[25] Schwartz, Gomes, and McCarthy suggest you follow your energy needs for sustainability (physical), self-expression (mental), significance (spiritual), and security (emotional)—and focus on meeting your needs in each area—so you are well-fueled and at capacity for delivering a stellar performance at whatever you are doing.

While we have become a fast-paced society, to be at capacity we must alternate between work and rest. We seem to have become a society that undervalues restoration and renewal—to our detriment. As a leader, you must show the way. People are following your lead. If you ignore rest, if you do not practice renewal strategies, others will think that is what you expect of them as well. You will be perpetuating the practices of overworking by teaching them to others.

What gives you energy? What gets you up in the morning? What are you passionate about? How do you recharge? What depletes or drains you? What frustrates, angers, or annoys you? These are all things that can help you learn how to be more effective at being human.

Notice your emotions about different things. Emotions offer you information; they are data providing you with a message. You just have to figure out what that message is communicating to you. Frustration, for example, is often described as wishing something were different. It is doing something in the same way and not achieving the result you seek, and that causes you to feel frustrated. Stop and assess— how might you need to change your approach, so you can achieve a different outcome? Disappointment refers to an unmet expectation. If you feel disappointed, explore your expectations. Were they realistic or reasonable, or were they unrealistic or unreasonable? What does that information tell you about how you might want to proceed?

Emotions are gateways to help us unravel pain and discomfort. Pleasant emotions provide a direction that makes us want to proceed; unpleasant emotions make us want to retreat or change course. Befriend your emotions. Pay attention to what you are feeling; sit with it and take a few minutes to name the feeling and decipher its meaning. Anger often means someone has trespassed a boundary. What happened? What boundary was crossed? Was that clear and known to the other person? How might you want to address that to ensure it does not happen again?

Being able to notice, name, and tame your emotional state is a skill that can be developed. At times, we can stop paying attention to what we are feeling for a number of reasons. We might talk ourselves out of our feelings, not notice, not pay attention, or minimize. Learn to pay closer attention to what you are feeling and what you are sensing in your gut. That information can be invaluable in navigating difficult situations.

Make a list of things that bother or frustrate you and start identifying ways that would clear them. Notice your emotions toward different people, projects, and things. Look at every area of your life and work including relationships, home life, physical health, mental health, spiritual health, and finances. If it is not exceptional and excellent, adding value to your life, giving you energy, or feeding your soul, then what would make it better? Why tolerate something that is mediocre or substandard? In the words of Jim Collins, "Good is the enemy of great." Many people settle for much less than good! If you are settling, if you are unhappy, or if something is mediocre, then address it. Don't settle for less than. What would make it better?

What Are You Avoiding?

When we avoid taking action, addressing difficult situations, making decisions, or taking a stand, are we leading? Our employees want their leaders to deal with the challenging stuff. This is what they look to us to do.

What gets in your way of taking firm and swift action? Some of my coaching clients report wanting to be nice. Fearing any type of confrontation, they would do anything to avoid upsetting people. One client stated that her strategy upon getting promoted was attempting to please people. It backfired. Her ability to actually provide leadership was severely hindered by a few people who felt entitled to whatever they thought was best for them. Hence, she decided to hire a coach to help her find other strategies that would be more effective to bring about change.

No one wants you to be nice. They want you to be real, to tell the truth, to do the right thing, to take a stand. Effective leaders develop the best in others and ensure everyone has a voice and that people treat others respectfully. This can be done with a team charter, team rules, or mutual agreements. As leadership expert and author Dr. John Maxwell often states, "A leader is one who knows the way, goes the way, and shows the way." People need leaders who can be decisive. Although it is wonderful and important to gain input from others, the leader often has a more expansive view, possessing knowledge of the organization's needs and strategies as well as the future vision. The leader needs to be able to synthesize information from many sources and then show people the path to success.

Another important growth edge for leaders is learning to manage difficult conversations. What tough conversations have you been avoiding? Worrying about having a tough conversation is often more stressful than addressing the issue and having the conversation. It does require skill. What resources do you need to address these difficult conversations?

What else are you avoiding? If you are avoiding something, are you leading? Leading effectively means facing difficult situations head-on. Your employees are counting on you to provide directions and clear the path. These difficulties cause people stress and make it harder to do the work. Your job as a leader is to reduce friction and eliminate those things that get in the way of your employees doing their best work. In what ways might you be making things more difficult than they need to be?

Another way people avoid is by staying busy. It is easier to just keep working than to feel the feelings of loss and pain or even gladness and joy. People avoid emotions when they are unskilled at feeling them and navigating them. But hiding in your work is not living. Hiding in your work means you are avoiding the other areas of your life—your home, your health, your relationships. Feeling our feelings is how we experience living. No one reaches the end of their life and wishes they had worked more. Scores of people interviewed at the end of their lives wished they had worked less, risked more, loved more, and forgiven more quickly.

Avoidance has a cost. You cannot know just how much better things can be until you face whatever it is that stands in the way. What might you need to face? What resources might be needed to help you work through this?

Expose Your Underlying Needs

What are some of the ways in which you get in your own way or sabotage yourself? These could be things like perfectionism, people-pleasing, needing to be in control, needing to be liked, or needing to be important or be recognized. Each of these has an underlying need associated with it and emotions attached to it and must be explored to address the underlying need directly.

Needs come from a lack in our lives as we were growing up. For example, perhaps as a small child, before you were able to clearly express yourself, you needed to be listened to, yet you heard, "Not now, I am busy" or "It better be important." As a result, you interpreted that to mean that no one listens to you, and you live your life assuming this as truth, that you will not be listened to. This construct can affect your relationships, your job, and how you approach others. A good way to change this is to replace your assumption with how you would like to be treated and make clear requests of others. Once a need is satisfied, it will no longer drive you.

Needs are not personal, although they certainly feel personal. They are not bad or wrong, and everyone has them. We are often unaware of our needs, however, so when we have an emotional need (are needy in some way), we tend to do things that are unhealthy to get the need satisfied. Our unmet needs can spill out through our behaviors. Needs must be satisfied, so if we are not in command of them, then they control us and our behaviors. Finding ways to identify our needs and have them met on our own terms empowers us to show up differently and is a skill set that can be developed.

There are different ways to recognize our needs. Emotions can clue us in to the presence of an unmet need. Another clue might be when you focus on yourself rather than the larger picture or other people. Our needs must be met for us to have space for others and be open to possibilities and alternative perspectives. When you hear yourself often using the words *me, myself, and I*, that could indicate the presence of an unmet need. Behaviors can also clue you in to the presence of an unmet need. By observing your behaviors and their impact, and by using your emotions to recognize when something you do does not quite feel right, you can become more aware of what might not be working well for you.

The goal is to identify your personal needs and then find healthy ways to get those needs satisfied. For example, one of my clients complained that her boss did not provide adequate feedback or validation of her work. She seemed to crave this and recognized it as an emotional need in order to feel better about her work. By recognizing this, she was able to look for other ways to get the need met, such as through colleagues and interactions with other leaders who often praised her and her work. She could also take some time to reflect on and acknowledge her own work. This gave her confidence, and she was able to move past the anger she was harboring toward her boss, who was not providing her with what she needed to feel successful in her role. In this way, she was able to get her needs met on her own terms rather than expecting someone else (the boss, in this case) to deliver something they were unable to do for her.

While we may have many personal needs, the need to be right is one of the most common and potentially the most damaging. Needing to be right can lead to conflict and often does, which increases our levels of stress. In fact, no wars have been waged, nor arguments fought, that were not a matter of differing points of view and someone needing to be right.

Needing to be right is different from *being* right. *Needing* to be right is an attachment to our ideas and the stories we tell ourselves. It is a function of the ego or our pride.

People often attach their value or self-esteem to their ideas. If you believe your value as a human being comes from your ideas, then what you hear when someone dismisses or disagrees with your ideas is not that your idea is wrong, but that *you* are wrong. You may become defensive as you try to defend your value as a human being. Think about your last argument—do you even remember what it was about? Most of the time, we cannot remember the topic, but we still remember how it felt.

More than anything, people want to feel valued. We want to make our point, be heard, and not feel like we are wrong or that our ideas don't count. Even if we are wrong, we don't know that. With information, knowledge, and our ability to synthesize that information, our conclusions seem right at the moment. People are right in their own minds. It takes a bit of skill to acknowledge what someone says about what they think and then add to it or express your own thoughts about the topic without making the person wrong in the process.

Needing to be right results in arguments, which can lead to relationship issues. It creates distance between people and decreases trust in relationships. When we put greater value on our ideas (our thoughts, conclusions, or assumptions) than we do on the relationship, we put up a wall that does not allow any incoming information. If we both get defensive, then the walls we put up bump against one another. No communication is getting through, and it feels bad. In essence, we stop listening and are unwilling to consider opposing ideas. And every time we do this, we must mend the relationship afterward—if mending it is possible.

If you find yourself in this type of situation, just stop. Pause for a moment and take a break to have the conversation at a later time. Or if you can calm yourself enough to shift your approach to the conversation, let the other person know that you are interested in what they have to say, you would like them to share their views, and then you would like to be given the time to share yours. If they agree to this arrangement, then you can have a productive conversation.

Peter Drucker, a consultant, educator, and author known for his philosophical and practical advancement of modern management theory, said, "We are here on earth to make a positive difference, not to prove how right or smart we are." You cannot possibly know it all or be right all the time. Practicing humility means focusing on *what* is right, rather than *who* might be right, and enables us to remain open to explore different viewpoints. It allows us to lead with our hearts, provides an opening for people to share themselves and their ideas, and increases trust and respect between parties. Often you will find that listening to other people's ideas provides additional information and perspectives that you may not have considered.

Is it so important to be right? Or is it more important to be a partner in the relationship and to demonstrate value for others? Be open to rethinking, to exploring possibilities, to entertaining new thoughts and different views. Be open to the best answer, not the one you thought of simply because you thought of it.

The Art of Listening

How well do you listen to others? Do you really hear them—what they are trying to convey with their words, body, and energy? Do you try to listen while multitasking? One of my clients realized through the coaching process that she spent an inordinate amount of time on tasks. She would get right down to business with people in meetings and rarely, if ever, took any time to get to know people on a personal level. People felt that she was abrupt and uncaring. They did not feel as though she heard them because she answered so quickly and did not seem to take any time to consider their point of view in her response.

Part of our work together was getting her to slow down and give people a chance to share what was on their minds before diving right in. Even if she knew the answer, allowing the other person to speak, understanding where they were coming from, and asking questions for clarification when appropriate changed the dynamic of her relationships. Over time, she realized that by not listening to people, she was missing out on building relationships. Not only did she not really get to know others, but they did not have a chance to get to know her. She wanted to change that.

People need to be seen and heard. This is one of the most respectful things we can do for another person. In fact, one reason coaching has become such a tremendous success is the art of listening. Often you may find that instead of listening well, other people try to fix you, tell you what to do, problem-solve for you, give advice, or change the topic and tell you their stories. People will often interrupt or focus on the answer rather than just listening and being fully present.

Active listening requires time and attention. It includes silence. It requires that you be fully present, without distractions. Listening requires that you pay attention to not only the words but the nonverbals too. What is this person really trying to communicate? They often don't know exactly. In the many years I have been teaching leadership, communication can be one of the most challenging topics, and yet it is so important to get it right. We are communicating all the time, and we often get it wrong.

Poor listening can become a huge source of stress for you and your employees. If you are not heard or if they are not heard, a divide is created, and you are not operating cohesively. It becomes impossible to produce the results you seek. Listening well saves time, decreases stress, increases respect and trust, and builds goodwill.

Good listening requires asking questions, being curious about what this person is trying to say, why they are saying it to you, and what they need from you. If you jump right into problem-solving, you may come up with solutions to the wrong problem. Most of the time, people don't need you to solve their problems; they need help clarifying the problem. How do they understand the situation? What is going on that is problematic? How did they come to this conclusion? Ask them to explain the situation, information or data they have collected, and how they came to their conclusions. The more time you spend asking questions to ensure the problem is clear, the easier it will be to identify the next steps.

Once you have clarified the problem, you can ask them what the challenge is *for them*. What part of this is giving them difficulty? Now that the problem is clarified, does that change how they see it? Do they see solutions more clearly as well?

What options or solutions have they identified? How else could this be handled? Spend time identifying new possibilities for action. What is the outcome they are looking for? What is their timeline? Who might be able to help with that? What help might they want or need from you?

Active listening is not about you. It is not about having a witty or quick answer. People do not need to be fixed. And although people may approach you with a problem, how do you know exactly what part of this situation they are struggling with? If you jump to problem-solving too fast, you lose the opportunity to listen and to help them think things through. Listening is an opportunity to help others think for themselves to develop critical thinking skills. You do not have the answers to someone else's riddle. You may be able to tell them what *you* would do, but you cannot tell people what *they* would do. They must figure that out for themselves. You can be a sounding board for them to do just that.

Listening well is a great skill to practice with everyone in your life—other leaders at various levels, your colleagues, friends, family, children, and spouse. Every person you meet is hungry to be heard and really listened to. Consider how you might develop better listening skills and the impact that will have on your reputation as a leader.

If you are always telling people what to do, you are not leading; you are instructing, teaching, directing, commanding. Listening requires coaching skills, and that includes the art of listening. The best thing you can do as a leader is to develop others, coaching them to be better versions of themselves. You are only as good as the people working for you, so help them be better—to think better. You do not always have to have the answers. Do you think you do?

Responding to Requests

Do you have difficulty saying no to requests for your time or talent? Just because you *can* do something, and do it well, does not mean you should do it. What are the thoughts or the story in your head associated with your saying yes to everything or your unwillingness to say no?

I've had clients who cannot say no because they feel guilty about telling a boss or colleague they will not do something for them. Some clients jump to say yes before giving adequate thought to what they are agreeing to and without first considering what they already have on their plate, what this would mean for their team, and whether it is a priority for them to handle. Other clients admitted they simply did not know how to say no or did not think they had a choice.

One client said yes to everything because she wanted to do all this stuff—it all seemed fun to her! However, not taking time to consider how much was on her plate, whether she had the bandwidth right now, whether the task was appropriate for her and aligned with her professional goals, and what taking it on would mean for her team meant that she was way too busy and overworking to the point of having no time to think or breathe. She had difficulty identifying priorities as there were so many projects that required her attention and oversight, and her team was impacted by her decisions due to the part they would have to play in achieving results and how little time she had to support them. She was stressed-out, and her team was also stressed-out.

Another client called this "death by a thousand paper cuts" as she was involved in way too many things and was doing way too much. She was all over the place. Spending time crafting her vision and mission helped her focus her efforts and made it easier to say no when the request was not aligned with her priorities. The simple exercises of identifying her vision, mission, and values were powerful for her as this meant she could go further faster with what she wanted to accomplish and eliminate the activities that did not align with it. This client gave herself a simple rule to follow: if the answer was a clear no, she could respond to that request right away; however, if the answer was a possible yes for her time, energy, and talent, she would wait twenty-four hours before giving an answer. This gave her time to pause, so she could check in with her vision and mission to determine whether the request was in alignment.

There is a lot here to unpack. Peel away the layers for yourself and look underneath the action. Is it that you cannot say no? Or is it that you like saying yes? Do you feel guilty about saying no? Do you feel the need to impress others or prove yourself? Are you concerned about how others will feel or what they will think of you? Do you just not know how to say no in a professional manner? Perhaps your culture has taught you that you should not turn down any request made by someone in authority. What is coming up for you here?

One client finally admitted that in her culture, she was taught never to turn down a request from a man, regardless of his position. Now that she was the leader over several men, she had to address this cultural rule that governed her behavior if she was to be successful in her role. She had to create new guidelines for herself, strategies that would honor her leadership role and would feel comfortable for her given her cultural heritage.

Being able to respond adequately and appropriately to requests for your time, energy, and talent, as well as to requests for your department's or team members' time and talents, is part of being an effective leader. It means managing your resources well. Your talent and the talents of your team are your assets, and they need to be managed just like any other asset. With the big picture in mind, what makes the most sense for the use of your resources? Who is the best person to do that work? Is now the right time? Once you uncover your hang-up about saying yes or no to requests, you can make better decisions about the use of your department's greatest asset—your human talent and resources.

Share the Work

How well do you delegate? If you are not delegating the work, are you leading? As the leader, you assume responsibility for a workload, and that workload gets distributed among the people who work for you. One of the biggest shifts we make when we step into leadership is the shift from individual contributor—a subject matter expert—to leader, where we are now responsible for the work of the team, department, or group.

If you struggle to delegate, explore what that is about for you. Do you fear losing control or that things will not be done well? Do you figure it is easier and faster to just do it yourself? One client said this to me during a recent session, and she admitted that she worked until late in the evening while her staff went home at a reasonable time. Every little thing that she was doing herself instead of delegating to others added to her workload. Just because you *can* do something does not mean you *should*.

Not delegating also sends a message to others about your level of trust. If you do not delegate work to someone whose job it is to do, that says something to them about how you feel about them and their ability to perform the job. It could be interpreted to mean that you don't trust them with the responsibility.

Do you feel guilty about giving work to others? One client admitted she felt guilty about "dumping" work on her team because everyone was so busy. By not giving people the work, however, she was not allowing them to develop and learn new skills, utilize their expertise, learn to organize and prioritize, and assume responsibility. Also, because she was assuming they could not handle the workload, she was not giving them the opportunity to discuss with her their workload and what they could handle. She was making assumptions about their ability without verifying the accuracy of those thoughts. This could mean she did not trust them. It could also mean that she did not want to relinquish control and was not being totally honest about her reasons for keeping the work to herself.

If you do not trust your team members to do the work, what might you do differently to build that trust? What would it take for you to feel comfortable turning over the work? What kind of training would be required for them to gain the skill or knowledge needed to perform the tasks? While it may take some time up front to train them to develop competency, it will save you time as they learn to do that work moving forward. What might you need to do to let go of your need to control?

There are different ways to delegate work, such as giving them parts of the work, having them do the research but not actually perform the work, having them do the work but verify it with you, or completely handing over the work to them without their needing to check in. Perhaps understanding the different levels of delegating and starting slowly with different people will help you learn the art of delegation while building trust and slowly relinquishing control as that trust develops.

Share the work—don't hoard the work. Being a leader means giving the work to the people and overseeing how it gets done, ensuring people have the necessary resources and training to be effective in their work. There will be things only you can do in your position—evaluations, hiring, strategizing, etc. Everything else that can be delegated, delegate. Trying to be the expert in all things means you wind up doing the work of others. That is not leading.

As director of nursing, one of the things I did when I arrived was look for things that were not working well. I identified several areas where we were bleeding money. One of those was the pharmacy bill. We were paying tens of thousands of dollars for the children's medications every month due to the lack of a prior authorization system. No one had taken responsibility for doing this in the past, so we were left with a huge bill every month for medications the children needed.

While I could have been the one to undertake this, it would have been a time-consuming endeavor, which would mean less time for me to perform other tasks that required my attention. I was able to identify a nurse on our team who was not only competent but who enjoyed tackling this project. She took it on and ran with it. She created a tracking system to ensure the medications were covered by their insurance, and she handled the ones that needed orders to be changed. She identified a few other nurses who could manage the process when she was out of the office or on vacation. What she needed from me was time away from the pressures of direct patient care so she could do this work, which I was able to provide. She saved us tens of thousands of dollars every month through her work. And I publicly praised her work to senior leadership whenever possible.

Rely on the expertise of others—encourage and support your people to grow in their expertise. Your job is to develop the people around you. Your success is based on how well you expand and grow the ability of others. Ask yourself, am I the best person for the job? If it does not need to be you specifically, then who is the best person for the job? If you are doing work that others can and should be doing, then you are not serving the organization well. You need to find ways to multiply yourself and maximize the efforts of those who report to you. In this way, you can lead more effectively and be fiscally responsible.

And What Else?

Being effective at leadership requires that you find your voice and speak up. This means offering suggestions and asking questions in meetings. It means trusting yourself and your own wisdom to make decisions and guide your people to success. What gets in the way of your being confident and self-assured?

Notice when you make excuses or rationalize about something. Notice when you feel fearful or lack the confidence or courage to take action or speak up for something you believe in. One of my clients shared that for the first two years in her leadership role, she listened to others tell her how to run the department, thinking they would have more wisdom and knowledge about how to best lead this group. It was a difficult group with some strong personalities.

However, after coaching for a few months, she started to realize that while others may have ideas for how they would lead this group, no one knew the group as she did. She was the one with a vision and a clear plan. She needed to give herself permission to take what she felt was the best course of action to develop the group members in the way they needed to grow. She had the instincts and ideas; she needed the courage to take the steps to make her vision a reality.

No one can tell you how to best lead in your context, given your experience and expertise. You are the one in the position. You were chosen for this role, and you know what is best. Sometimes it just takes a good coach or listener to pull what you already know out of you, so you can do the very things you know you should do.

Notice any resistance you may have. Resistance can point to fear you may be harboring. In what ways are you hiding or holding back your brilliance? What might you be minimizing or failing to address?

Consider your mindset and your relationship to risk or possibility. Do you tend to be risk averse and have difficulty being optimistic and considering possibility? Are you overly positive or optimistic and unable to see the risks? There is value in both—being risk averse as well as being positive and considering possibilities. Listening to how others view certain projects or plans can help you avoid unnecessary risk, consider other options as well as consequences, and see possibilities where you may not be looking.

Another problem many people have is overthinking. Is this a problem for you? Do you get lost in detail, overthink things, or become overly analytical? What impact does this have on your ability to lead effectively and make decisions?

One client discussed how she would overshare and provide a lot of detailed information to validate her decision and ensure the person understood how she came to that conclusion. When we unpacked this, she was able to identify that she did this to prove herself knowledgeable, which helped her establish her confidence. Once she realized this was what she was doing, she was able to find better ways to communicate—more simply, succinctly, and with confidence. She had the authority to make these decisions, she was knowledgeable, and she always did her due diligence; there was no need for her to explain (or overexplain) herself. She was the expert and had the authority to make the best decision for the organization without providing an extended explanation. This was a big shift for her.

When you are stressed at work, how does that impact on your personal life and your relationships outside of work? You go with you wherever you go. The ways in which you show up at work will show up in other areas of your life as well. Being more willing to explore yourself—the ways you think, how you feel, the reasons you do the things you do, and what you might want to do differently—will help you become more effective at leading yourself and, therefore, leading others.

To read more about self-exploration and becoming more self-aware and confident, you might find my other book, *The Journey Called YOU: A Roadmap to Self-Discovery and Acceptance*, to be informative.[26]

The Trade-off

If you say yes to one thing, the consequence is that you will not have the time or energy for something else. You cannot be in two places at once. When you say yes to something, what are you saying no to? And when you say no to something, what are you then able to say yes to? Imagine the possibilities. There is always a trade-off. This requires you to consider your priorities and values, so you can make the best decisions for your time, energy, and talent.

When I became a director, there was so much to do. Things seemed so chaotic, and the department needed structure, planning, and organization. After a few years, I came to realize that I had been running at 100 miles an hour and I was suffering. I was always "on." The work got done, but my relationships were suffering. I was so busy doing stuff that I did not have the time or make the time for others. I was enjoying my work, but I was not happy. I was moving too fast, and life seemed to be passing me by.

I decided that I needed to slow down, and that became my theme (a mantra if you will). It took me several years to figure out what that meant for me, and in some ways, I am still learning. I had to revisit my priorities and my values so they could be my guides. I have always been someone who liked to work hard, keep things (or get things) organized, and stay on top of trends and issues. I had bought into the societal belief—the big LIE—that work is supposed be hard, it should look a certain way, and I had to put so much pressure on myself to be good enough. No one else was pressuring me to push myself in the way I had been pushing. I was doing this to myself.

In the end, I realized that this way of thinking, this mindset, was hurting me. I had to learn to do things differently, to approach work differently. It took me several years to downshift and let go of the stress and craziness, to identify the ways in which I get in my own way, and to remain steadfast and in a state of calm and peace. I don't want to be overwhelmed, I don't want crazy, and I don't want to have any added stressors in my life. Life is stressful enough without adding stress or drama to it unnecessarily.

I want peace. And I want connection. I want to add things to my life that feel good. And I want to live my values and play to my strengths every day.

In addition to the stressors we face at work, many things outside of work impact us: relationship stressors, medical issues, spiritual distress, financial stress. Children, elderly parents, or other family members can be sources of added stress. Many things can impact us and how we might approach our work. You go with you wherever you go, so if something in your life is amiss you are carrying it, even if you are trying your best to compartmentalize. You still feel the stress and the strain, and that can affect your productivity and performance.

Notice your feelings throughout your day and try to identify the stressors and their impact on how you show up and perform at work. The more aware you are, the more capable you become of making choices that serve you better. That is both empowering and liberating.

As you move up in the organization, and as you gain awareness, control over your mind, and start to act differently, you become more influential. You have more of an ability to impact those organizational stressors, to reduce them and create a better work environment for your team. This prepares you for the next bigger/better thing, where you are needed and can make an even bigger/better contribution to the organization and others. With more awareness and self-control, you lead with greater confidence and communicate with more assertiveness. You learn how to lead effectively and be a better role model, even to higher-ups who may want what you have. You will start to attract people, things, projects, and opportunities.

Fill Your Cup

If you drain yourself with the many different ways you stress yourself out, how will you have any energy left for the other important parts of your life? In Stephen Covey's highly acclaimed book *The 7 Habits of Highly Effective People*, we learned that we have to "sharpen the saw," or renew ourselves regularly so that we have the energy and ability to serve others.[27] After all, Covey shared, "You cannot cut with a dull knife."

There is so much information available about self-care—the importance of sleep, nutrition, resilience, healthy relationships—all the wonderful things that help you and your body to perform your best. What do YOU need to be your best? What is the best nighttime routine? When is the best time for you to wake up? What is your exercise or movement routine and when do you complete that? What do you do to connect with others, to love, to be generous, to play and have fun?

Give yourself permission to say yes to you. Without you, what do you have? Say no to what is not an effective use of your time. Say yes to the things that matter. If you do not put yourself first, who will? Who will take care of you if you don't?

Dream about what a less-stressed life would be like. If you can see it and feel it and believe in the possibility of it, you can create it. This is not easy to accomplish; stress is what we are used to. It is our mode of operating! And often it is what we see other people doing. We struggle to change. That does not mean we can't change, but it requires attention, commitment, and consistent action. As a leader, you go first. You show the way to a new way of approaching work.

Inward first. We do our own work first. Slow down. Be present in this moment. And notice yourself—your thoughts, feelings, beliefs, and stories. Notice and name them—then choose your response. That is what we can control. Then we can turn our attention outward to how we can support others in being their best at work.

In the next chapter, we will explore the organizational stressors that have an impact on you as well as your staff and identify ways to decrease stress and reduce the friction that others face. We can use our positional power to create a better place for people to work.

CHAPTER 6

Create a Respectful
Work Environment

> *Leadership is about making others better*
> *as a result of your presence and making*
> *sure that impact lasts in your absence.*
>
> —SHERYL SANDBERG

I was speaking with one of my nurses who had just returned from vacation. She stated that although she had a fabulous time away, she was glad to be back. She loved her work and enjoyed returning to the job first thing on a Monday morning. This made my heart sing.

I always believed that my role as leader meant it was my responsibility to create a work environment that worked—where people enjoyed practicing their craft and working with one another on the team and where they had the resources they needed to do their jobs well. While I had no control over the work itself, I could focus attention on making the place run in a way that supported excellence in nursing care. If my nurses enjoyed working with adolescents in a psychiatric environment, then together we could create a workplace where people enjoyed coming to work.

As a leader, you have the opportunity to influence change. Things you struggled with as an individual contributor can ignite your passion for helping change the systems for others to make a better workplace. By reducing friction, we look for ways to make it easier for people to do their jobs and do them well. This could mean providing resources, training, staff, scheduling options—whatever we can find to remove barriers and smooth the path for people to do their work.

In the last chapter, we explored ways in which we were causing stress for ourselves and how that might be impacting our productivity and affecting others. In this chapter, we will explore organizational stressors and identify things that get in the way, slow things down, or cause frustration. This means excavating and looking for things that make the work harder than it needs to be, then finding ways to make things work more efficiently and effectively. Identifying and reducing the organizational stressors helps reduce the stress for yourself and your staff, prevents burnout, and helps people thrive at work, making retention and recruitment easier. People will want to be there and will want to perform at their best.

This is the fun part of leadership. It is one reason to delegate work to others who are capable of doing it well. That frees you to use your time and your wider perspective to identify areas of stress and challenge. Then you can work to find ways to eliminate anything that impedes the good work of others. This is using your leadership power for good, and it impacts the bottom line in ways that are often hard to measure.

When I became a nursing director, some nurses wanted me to pass out meds and provide direct care to the children. I resisted this and explained that if I did that job, who would do mine? They had a skewed perception of what a leader was supposed to do. Previous managers either worked with the patients alongside the nursing staff or were completely absent and inaccessible to them. They had little idea of what their leader should or could be doing for them. I had to teach them and show them through my words and actions what my role was—it was to make it a better place to work, to advocate for their needs as well as the needs of the patients, and to ensure they had the resources needed to do their jobs well (equipment, staffing, salaries, etc.).

Someone had to represent the nursing voice at meetings. Someone had to take a stand and ensure the nurses had what they needed to do their work. It took some time, but eventually they understood. And this did not mean I never helped out directly with the patients. At times there were not enough nurses to do the work and I had to step in. But the staff then knew that the department was lacking support if I was not doing the work of leading.

In this chapter, we will start by identifying things that might be stress producing, then explore things that can deplete the energy of people at work. Your job as leader, should you choose to accept it, is to reduce friction for others where you can. We end the chapter exploring those things that cannot be changed, where you have no control, but where you might acknowledge and connect with your staff so that you can ride those storms out together.

Clear the Path

Creating a positive and healthy work environment, where people feel comfortable and engaged at work, requires that you create structure, define expectations, and communicate a clear vision, as well as connect with your people and care about them (we will cover this topic in Part III). To create what you and your employees need to thrive in the workplace requires that you also remove things that do not add value, things that get in the way and hold people back from bringing their best selves to work.

Organizational issues can be energy depleting and stress producing, causing your employees to become disengaged, disgruntled, and burned-out—and potentially even quiet quit or seek new employment. As a leader, you have some authority to improve conditions for others. You can be the beacon of hope. First, you must uncover the stressors sneaking into your workplace.

What is it like to work in your department or organization? How does it feel? Do people care about each other? Do they support and encourage one another? How are the newly hired brought on board? What is that experience like? Do your staff welcome newcomers? Do your teams have clear values and team rules of conduct? Is the work environment respectful?

Culture plays a crucial role in how people feel in the workplace and whether they are engaged or struggling. Many problems and stressors are present in organizations. Your job is to locate these and do whatever you can to fix them. Pay attention to how people feel at work. Ask about their greatest challenge. Look for and listen to people's complaints—they may not express themselves clearly, but they will tell you what you need to know, if you listen and ask better questions. Sift through the employee surveys. Go out there and talk to your people. If you listen to the people and if you can gain their trust, they will tell you everything you need to know about what is working and what is not.

Inadequate management shows up in many different ways. You might find that strategies or objectives are unclear. If people do not know what is expected of them, how can they possibly produce it? People will do the best they can with the information they have. If you give them a lemon and provide no instructions, can you fault them for making lemonade instead of slicing the lemon into slivers? Often this is exactly what happens, and the wrong outcome is blamed on the individual, who ends up with a poor year-end evaluation. A lack of clarity and uncertainty about what is expected translates into stress, frustration, and poor morale, which can lead to absenteeism and turnover, and poor or incorrect outcomes for the organization, all of which impact the bottom line. It's a lose-lose proposition.

Communication is often a challenge in organizations, whether it is clarity of expectations or providing appropriate information. Not having correct or sufficient information to do one's job is stressful. When people do not communicate well, do not collaborate well, and do not share enough information, people cannot do their jobs well.

They may achieve results, but those may not be the results needed or desired.

Incompetent people in positions of power wreak havoc among employees and create toxic, unhealthy work environments. There are obvious examples such as abusive bosses, economic abuse (giving people more responsibility or even a title without adequate compensation), bullying, or lateral violence. When it is ever acceptable to yell at another person? How is that ever professional?

Lateral violence is a form of displaced violence, where anger is directed at members of an oppressed community, such as new hires or new graduates. It could be expressed as gossip, blaming, shaming, ignoring an individual, not providing adequate information to perform their work, threatening, or intimidation. These behaviors create a toxic or hostile work environment. Such violent behavior does not have to be physical; it is often emotional or mental abuse or even neglect. This is inexcusable. It is a leadership problem.

Bullying and lateral violence are a lot more common in the workplace than you would think. Although commonplace in healthcare, lateral violence can be experienced in any industry or workplace. From corporate America to the small family business, there are mean, nasty behaviors that take place on a regular basis meant to humiliate and beat people down. These behaviors can also be experienced at home. How you behave in one place is typically how you behave wherever you are because of the thoughts that are motivating this reaction.

In stressful environments where tempers and egos flare, it can be hard to maintain composure and think clearly to remain professional. And yet that is exactly what needs to happen. If violence of any kind exists, it is the fault of the leader who tolerates it. You are in a position to change that and to move toward a work environment that is respectful and considerate. As you create a healthier workplace, people will learn new behaviors and take those behaviors with them into their homes and communities. This is how we can change the world.

There is no excuse for bad behavior at work. Having to deal with a boss, coworker, or other professional whose behavior is inappropriate, aggressive, hostile, or nasty triggers the stress response and causes people to be on edge. Walking on eggshells at work is never healthy and impedes people's ability to produce their best work. Stress results in an inability to access the higher functioning of the brain and reduces creativity and intelligence. If you want people to do their best work, then your goal as a leader is to reduce the fear and stress that people experience at work.

Incidents do happen. As much as you try to prevent it, people do have outbursts and stressors get the better of them. There are also people who take out their issues on others. What matters most is how you deal with things as they come up. What are the rules for managing the bad behavior of others in your organization? What is your plan for handling these things when they occur? What matters most to your team is what you do and how quickly you manage it.

In my time as an executive, I was very clear about what was expected. People were treated respectfully, as professionals. We did have a nurse who tended to bully others, typically the newer, younger, or quieter nurses. Because the nurses spent a good bit of time in their respective workstations, my leadership team never witnessed this behavior. Luckily, we had created an environment where the staff felt comfortable approaching me to discuss the issues they were experiencing. I was glad they felt safe reporting their problems and trusted me to make things better. I took their complaints seriously and promptly dealt with any complaint I received. And the staff expected me to ensure that the behavior stopped, especially given my guiding principle for respect and professionalism. They held me accountable to uphold my own standards.

We also experienced a physician problem. This one was tricky. I actually got annoyed with my staff for not informing me sooner. My rule was that if something was amiss or did not feel right, they needed to inform me. We would discuss it and see how we could better handle it. I always emphasized that my role was to make their life at work as easy as possible. I could not change the work, but it was my job to ensure a positive work environment. But I could not help them if I did not know about the problem.

Evidently, this doctor mistreated the staff regularly. She was nasty and belittling and generally treated them with an air of contempt. Although I would often visit when the physician was working, she did not misbehave in my presence. I did not know of the problem until she mistreated a patient by being condescending and uncaring. The nurse called me immediately, very upset about how the child had been treated. This set off an investigation where I learned more about this physician's ongoing poor behavior to the nurses. Sometimes, when people gain (perceived) power, in this case, the doctor to the nurse, they can abuse that power, believing they are better than others.

I spoke with the physician leader and made it clear that the behavior would not be tolerated and that either there would be specific guidelines for this physician to follow or else we did not need her to tend to our children. Ultimately, it was decided that this physician would not return to our campus.

As the leader, I was responsible for ensuring the safety of both the children in our care and the staff. It took courage to stand up for what is right, rather than be intimidated by the power of the physician.

I had spent many years studying leadership and had been coaching leaders for over a decade before accepting this leadership position. My role as a leader was clear to me—to ensure the well-being of those in my care, and that included my staff as well as the patients. Given the power of my position, I had the opportunity as well as the responsibility to create a great place to work, where my staff could thrive. There was no reason to accept inappropriate behavior. However, addressing it does require courage. If you don't, it will continue to occur. And if someone misbehaves in one place, they will do it elsewhere. So, if a staff member raises their voice or talks offensively to another staff member, for example, they will also do this to a customer, patient, or family member. How you do one thing is typically how you show up everywhere.

This means that if someone mistreats you, and you are in a leadership role, they are doing the same thing to those who work with them. Others may be more intimidated or unable to speak up for themselves. Regardless of how you feel about the person, the difficult conversation you now need to have, or how fearful or intimidated you may be, you have an obligation to deal with it, not just to honor yourself but to ensure that the person does not treat anyone else in that manner.

As a leader, you are responsible for ensuring that people feel safe at work, especially from each other. A team charter or team rules help define the standards for how people are expected to behave, to treat each other, and even to define how conflict will be managed. One way to eliminate or reduce issues between staff is to make all of those unwritten rules of conduct explicit. Review them with your team and write down what you have all agreed to. Revisit them from time to time. Having these rules or mutual agreements ensures that everyone knows what is expected of them.

Stressors abound in organizations. Leaders need to be on guard and keep a lookout for challenges their staff may be facing. For example, when people are not afforded the appropriate level of authority and must ask permission to obtain approval, this not only adds stress but also costs the organization time and slows things down. Giving the power to the lowest level in the organization, those closest to the customer or product, can aid in smoothing and streamlining how things are completed and how decisions are made. The people closest to the customer or product are the very people with the most information.

Another stressor is giving staff adequate decision-making authority without allowing them to make mistakes. If people must be perfect all the time and are admonished—especially publicly—when things do not turn out well, this creates a lot of stress. If people can't ever be wrong, I guarantee mistakes and errors are happening all the time without you knowing it. People will hide their mistakes from you, and they will be scared to tell you when things are not going as planned.

How you handle mistakes or problems as a leader is an important part of creating a great team that works well together.

Do your employees have enough training and resources? Are there enough employees to perform the expected work? Assess the leaders.

Do they take credit for other people's work, or are they celebrating their workers? These factors create stress for your employees, especially when their basic needs are not met.

Anytime employees must walk on eggshells with certain people; carefully expend time and energy navigating difficult bosses; work without adequate support, equipment, or training to do their jobs well; or do not feel safe to speak up, be innovative, or make mistakes, this increases their stress levels and decreases their well-being at work. Having to shrink or hide in some way, being unable to be yourself and share all you have to offer the world, is stressful, disengaging, and unproductive.

All of this is unnecessary and preventable. And it is costly to the organization in the form of attrition, poor morale, low productivity, lack of creativity and innovation, and increased use of absenteeism and sick time. Providing adequate support and resources matters. Clear communication makes a significant impact. Respect matters. Autonomy and control over one's work is motivating and energizing. In fact, lack of control is a huge stressor. So wherever and whenever you can give people control, this will decrease stress and increase engagement. Muster your courage and take a stand for doing what is right, for enabling employees to perform at their best and create great outcomes for your organization.

Reduce Friction

Your job as a leader is to reduce friction and make it easier for people to perform their jobs. You have power in your position to impact others in a positive way. Find ways to make the lives of your employees easier.

In the sport of curling, one player pushes a large puck (called a stone) on ice down the court toward a target (like a bull's-eye) while another player (or two) sweeps the ice in front of the puck with brooms to decrease the friction, allowing the stone to travel a straighter path and move faster. This analogy is what we as leaders are to do for our staff—make it easier and faster for them to perform their best work. Identifying and providing what your staff need to succeed—such as training, resources, clear communication, and development opportunities—and eliminating what gets in the way of productivity—such as too many demands, long hours, pay disparities, and lack of equipment or direction—are ways you reduce friction.

One day I arrived at the main nursing station to find a nurse looking for a piece of equipment she needed to care for a child. She wondered which nurse had used it last, so she could determine which nursing station to visit.

We had five nursing stations on that campus. If she was spending time searching each nursing station to find something that could be at any one of them, that was an example of friction—a waste of time and energy and a source of frustration and stress. It was also an opportunity cost, which meant that while she was searching for the equipment, she was not providing care or able to be of service to the children she was assigned.

Each nursing station should be equipped with the tools necessary for the nursing staff to be able to perform their duties. This is called redundancy, meaning that there should be enough equipment at each of the nursing stations to provide care for the children in that building. No one should be running around campus trying to find something.

To decrease the friction and make it easier for the nurses to do their work, I instructed the staff to order what they needed so that each station could be adequately and completely equipped. Expensive equipment would be shared and housed at the main nursing station; however, all smaller and regularly used items needed to be made redundant.

They were a bit startled at first. They were accustomed to running around searching for items. Having plenty of what was needed was a new way of thinking about their workplace since that type of support was not provided by previous leaders. Once the staff understood that they could order what was needed to perform their job duties effectively and efficiently, it became much easier for them to provide high-quality care. It saved them time and reduced the frenzy and frustration. It also meant we had backups in case something broke or malfunctioned. And although I could not measure it directly, I knew this resulted in cost savings to the organization even though initially it required some expense to obtain the equipment needed.

Providing adequate resources was one way I built trust with my staff. Trust reduces friction because it enables you to get more done faster.

How might you reduce friction for your team? What stresses out your staff? What keeps them up at night? Have you asked them? What resources do they need to perform their duties? Are you ensuring they have what they need?

What stresses out your boss? What about your colleagues? What might you do to alleviate or reduce their stress through your work or department?

One way to uncover stress at work is to perform skip level interviews. This is where you interview the people who report to the managers who report to you. It is a way for you to learn what is going on at the front lines and assess how the managers are doing.

One of my clients, Caleb (not his real name), was a longtime information technology (IT) director. He had been working with one of his managers on an issue involving one of her direct reports who was not performing his job as expected. While others were responding to calls and emails to the tune of three hundred actions a month, this employee only handled maybe ten. For a year, no one had been able to calculate this data until a system was put in place that provided that level of detail.

How could this have gone undetected for so long? Did this employee understand the expectations of his position? Did his peers cover for him, or did no one notice that he was not doing the work? Were there team meetings to discuss the work and how things were going? Did anyone ever meet with him individually to determine how he was doing, review expectations and output, and set goals? How was that information explored? Perhaps the manager, who was new, did not know how to assess her employees and their output or how to create a team. However, that was Caleb's job—to ensure that the manager knew how to oversee her people.

With data in hand, they were able to meet with the employee and set clear expectations for the amount of work he was expected to deliver. Luckily for them, this employee obliged without incident. The outcome is not always that positive. For my client, however, the work for him as the director was to determine ways to explore the output of the employees in his division and ensure they were all working to their capacity and had a full understanding of the nature of the work to be done.

Your role as a leader is to help people be successful, be part of the team, and perform great work so that the team can produce great outcomes for the organization. It requires oversight. In fact, that is the leader's role: oversight. Individual contributors do the work that needs to be done, while leaders assess how everyone's work is coming together to achieve the department's success.

This requires getting to know your staff, providing feedback and training, finding ways to give them added responsibility, using their gifts and talents, and determining their goals for development so you can help them grow and excel. Developing your people is part of your role as leader. People want to be challenged at work. They want to be stretched. They want responsibility and the autonomy and control necessary for making decisions in their area.

As previously discussed, leaders must be aware of the demands placed on their employees and notice when those demands are causing stress and strain. When job demands or stressors are high, this can impact satisfaction experienced on the job. What mitigates the demands placed on people at work is the ability to act autonomously and have the freedom to control their work.[28] Considerable research has been done in this area. When demands are high, yet control or autonomy is low, employees experience an increased stress level and all the negative effects that go along with that—attrition and turnover, poor morale, decreased productivity, and increased absenteeism and use of sick time.

Where might you be able to give more control and autonomy to others?

Demands and stress also come from the individual themselves—how they think, their approach to work, how well they care for themselves, and stressors outside of work that they carry with them. We all have stressors outside of work that we need to deal with. We may be raising children and caring for loved ones, elderly parents, or perhaps a partner or spouse. We may have relationship issues or be lacking relationships.

Other stressors might include physical issues such as disabilities or medical conditions—ours or a family members. We all have finances to manage and bills to pay. There are spiritual and emotional challenges we must all face as well. People harbor grief and loneliness, deal with mental health issues such as anxiety and depression, lack confidence, or struggle with self-esteem. Consider things from your own life that you are dealing with. You cannot know what another person is managing.

People carry many things with them from their past into the present as well as their fears about the future. And although many people like to say they can separate their work life from their home life, compartmentalizing is only possible to a point. You go with you wherever you go, and you take your emotions, struggles, beliefs, and angst with you. The more work you do on yourself—becoming more aware, asking for what you need, and navigating the difficult emotions and situations that life presents to you—the more capable you are of empathizing with others and recognizing how they may be struggling at work.

One of our nurses, who I'll call Celeste, loved to work and often picked up overtime. She picked up so much overtime that at one point she had scheduled herself fourteen days in a row! When I spoke with her about it, we discussed the importance of rest and recovery. I cared about her. I also cared about the children in our care. To be a good team member, we each needed to have a life outside of work that included time to rest and rejuvenate. Whatever her reasons for wanting to work every day, and despite our need to fill the shifts with staff, I cared enough for her that I had to ensure she took time for herself away from work and the daily stressors we faced.

Everything presented to you in your life offers lessons and opportunities for your own growth. I have experienced a lot of bad leadership along my journey, and it has led me to learn and grow in many ways because of who I am and what I believed was possible and appropriate in leadership. In many respects I would never treat another human being the way I was treated or witnessed others being treated. That is kind of sad when I think about it. But those experiences informed my approach to leadership and helped me define how I wanted other people to feel when they worked for or with me.

Set People Up for Success

I mentioned in chapter 1 that when I began my role as director of nursing, I received limited onboarding. I was provided limited training on the software programs we used and did not have access to all the digital files needed to do my work (of course, I did not know this until someone asked me to look something up and we realized the problem).

Do you have a similar sad story of not being onboarded adequately while being expected to perform a job without the appropriate direction or instruction? I have found over the years of speaking with other professionals and leaders that they, too, have such stories.

After spending a few months in the role, I learned that the prior director had not made the effort to connect with people, especially those with a lesser title, who reported feeling that she was condescending and demanding. Staff reported that they had no direct relationship with the prior leader, who provided no direction, feedback, or support and often did not answer her phone if they needed something.

The nursing department was bleeding money, overspending the budget by hundreds of thousands of dollars annually. Procedures required for accreditation were lacking. Performance evaluations had not been prepared for several years. I wondered what work the previous leader actually delivered and what value she provided since many of her responsibilities were not completed.

My job was to unravel the mess: what was done and working well, what was not done and needed to be put into place, what areas needed improvement, and what could be scrapped altogether. Where could we save money? What procedures were lacking? How were the staff doing? What did they enjoy? What did they need? What were their challenges? I intended to evaluate and organize the department, regain control of the finances, and create a healthy and positive work environment where the nurses could enjoy their work with the children in our care. I also had to define the type of leader I would be and how I would elicit the support I needed to accomplish all the things I wanted to do.

This situation challenged me in so many ways—strategizing and looking at the big picture, asking for help, developing strong boundaries, dealing with difficult personalities, managing tight resources, asserting myself, navigating conflict, and clearly defining what I stood for as well as standing up for myself, my team, and my values. I had to learn to communicate effectively to different audiences, set clear expectations, hold people accountable, and connect with people at all levels of the organization.

Adversity shows you what you are made of and gives you the opportunity to be strong, find yourself, and grow your capacity. While I found the ability and developed the capacity to do great things in this role, I was not set up for success. I was set up for stress.

My initiation into the role was stressful! And it certainly tested the limits of my resilience. Intuitively, I knew I was in the right place and that I would find a way. I knew what needed to be done, and I was committed to making it happen. I wanted to lead this department well, and I wanted to create the best possible work environment for the staff who were so dedicated to the kids in our care. While I could not change the work or the challenges we faced, I could make the workplace one where people enjoyed working together and practicing their craft.

My experience was not something I ever wanted anyone else to endure. I was in a position to ensure that no one else would ever be treated that way in my department. We arranged for a thorough orientation for any newly hired nursing staff. With assistance from some of the nurses, we created an orientation guide, which included the most essential information required to function at a minimal level to provide care for our patients. It was printed and also placed online for any nurse to access. It reflected several of our most commonly used procedures, phone numbers, and timetables for the medication schedules. We also regularly reviewed and updated the guide and sought feedback from our new hires to ensure it enabled them to succeed in their duties.

How do you onboard your staff? How do people know what to do, where to go, and who they need to connect with? How might you be setting people up for stress rather than success? When you consider your leadership style, how can you make it easier to support your team members, bring out the best in them, and provide a work environment where people can thrive?

Ask questions. Be curious about what it is like to work for you and your team. Is there bullying? Are people kind and respectful? What is it like for a new employee to get started? What training is offered? How do you ensure that people have the necessary resources to do their jobs well? How will you develop and motivate your people?

The well-being of your staff is your responsibility. While you cannot be responsible for people's wellness or how they treat themselves, you are responsible for the demands you make, your behaviors, and the stressors you place on others.

Add Value

Make the organization a better place for your having been there. What mark will you leave?

We have all seen the words "I was here" scribbled on trees and in bathroom stalls, among other places. Perhaps you even left a mark somewhere like that when you were young. What was the point of doing that? Why was it important to inform others that you were there?

We announce ourselves because we want to matter. We want to be seen. We want to belong. We want to feel good for having lived or contributed or been part of making the world a better place.

You will leave your mark on others as you travel your life journey, and you will leave an imprint on others from being in this position and in the organization. Your presence, actions, words, and outcomes will create an impact. What is the impact you want to have on others, on the department, on the organization? What do you bring to the organization to make people better and make the organization better? How would you like to be remembered? What will your legacy be when you leave the organization?

We have been discussing the importance of reducing friction and making work life easier for people to be able to perform their job duties. Another important strategy for leaders is to add value. If reducing friction is about reducing the hindrances and bottlenecks, clearing the path to productivity, then adding value is about increasing the positives: bringing energy, direction, and thoughtfulness, and ensuring that people understand how valuable and important they are to the success of the team and the organization. Adding value is about lifting people up, giving them hope, and instilling a positive, healthy atmosphere in the workplace. It is about what you create with your presence and your activities.

It can be stressful and energy depleting to have to deal with ineffective staff, poor leadership, a lack of resources, unsuitable training, bad behaviors, lateral violence, or unclear expectations. It can also be stressful and exhausting when there are not enough positive and healthy things that add value and that feel good at work. These include compliments, recognition, and acknowledgment; appropriate challenges and responsibilities; autonomy over the work; constructive feedback; opportunities to gain experience and develop; and even opportunities to connect with others, collaborate, and work as part of a team.

Psychologist Frederick Herzberg described this phenomenon in his motivator-hygiene theory. He stated that there is a set of basic factors that is required or expected at a workplace. These factors include things like salary, supervision, working conditions, security, adequate workspace, and relationships with peers. Employers provide these basic factors, called hygiene factors, to employees to ensure that people will at least not be dissatisfied at work. These are the minimal requirements necessary for comfortable working conditions, but they are not necessarily motivating. No one is skipping for joy over working conditions or workspaces.

Other factors, however, can create job satisfaction and be very motivating. These motivating factors include things like achievement, recognition, the work itself, and opportunities for growth and advancement.

Leaders must pay attention to the basics as well as the motivating factors to avoid creating dissatisfaction among employees and to create conditions that stimulate job satisfaction. While you may not be able to influence some of these factors, you can focus on what you control in your area of leadership, starting with your presence and the atmosphere you create around you.

Your presence should add value to those you serve. How do people feel when they interact with you? What is the experience you want people to have when you interact? When you walk into a room, what do people think and feel? How are you viewed?

Maya Angelou is known for having said, "People won't remember what you said, but they will remember how you made them feel." It is important to consider the experience people have when interacting with you in some way.

I remember when I first started working as a floor nurse in the psychiatric hospital. The staffing coordinator would post the schedule on her door, so everyone could discover which unit they would be working for that shift. People would gather around the schedule and discuss the other people they would be working with. The things they said were not always kind. I remember thinking I never wanted to be that person who people would say negative things about. I wanted to be the person that people were glad to see on the schedule and looked forward to working with. I tried my best to be the kind of nurse people felt confident in—someone who was a good team player that they trusted to provide leadership, effective communication, direction, and support.

Become self-observant and reflect on the following questions honestly. How do people respond to your presence? Are people glad to see you in meetings, or do they sigh with relief when you leave? Do people listen to you? Do they want to hear what you have to say, or are they glad when you stop talking? What do you see and hear from others in daily conversation that imparts ideas about who you are to them and how they feel about you?

You may discount the little things said to you, like an acknowledgment for a job well done, comments made about your work, or whether you are missed if you are away from work for a while. All these things matter in identifying what you mean in the lives of others. In fact, the little things matter the most. Take notice of the things said to you and compliments given to you. Learn to receive them graciously. You cannot know what you mean to others unless they tell you how you have impacted them. Recently, I received a message online from an old boyfriend's sister who—all grown up and married now—shared that she often thinks of me and the impact I had on her during that time, that I was like a sister to her. I never knew that. What a gift to know that I made this impact on her!

All feedback is a gift. We cannot see ourselves as others do, so we require others to share with us their perspective. And we must be open to hear it, to receive it, and to express gratitude to the person sharing it. What a beautiful way to connect with another human being.

While feedback is another person's perception of you, it is still their experience. Not right, wrong, good, or bad—just an experience. Feedback can help you uncover blind spots. Blind spots are awareness gaps and are parts of yourself that you cannot see or access but need someone else to point out to you. That is why they are called blind spots!

Because feedback is the other person's perspective, it belongs to them. So, if you shrug it off or do not receive it well (whether the feedback is positive or constructive), it is as if you are telling them that their perspective is wrong. It feels uncomfortable to give a compliment to someone who refuses to accept it. It can feel as though the person giving it is wrong for having this experience or opinion, and people don't want to be wrong.

Receive feedback with grace. One way to do this is to lean into the feedback by asking the person to tell you more. "Tell me more about how I impacted you." You are asking for that person's viewpoint. It is not truth, but it is a perspective from someone else's vantage point. You do not have that viewing platform. By asking them to share, you gain information about yourself that you could not know otherwise.

As you move up the leadership ladder, it becomes even harder to get honest feedback. Often this is where having a coach can be instrumental for a leader's development. The coaching relationship could be the only place where a leader can speak openly and honestly and explore their thinking to be able to expand their perspectives.

Along with self-reflection, gaining information about yourself from others is essential for increasing your self-awareness. In her book *Insight*, Tasha Eurich shared her research on self-awareness.[29] Eurich described how self-awareness requires both internal self-awareness, which is clarity around how we see ourselves, and external self-awareness, or how others see us. To be truly self-aware, we need to access more than just our own reflection on how we show up. Eurich's research also found that most people are not as self-aware as they think they are. The good news is that we can improve.

How you lead impacts the work environment. You set the tone and others respond to your lead—and your mood. When you are angry, other people feel it. They may avoid you. If you are emotionally reactive, people have learned ways to work around your behaviors, including shrinking, hiding, or even quitting. You cannot obtain people's best work when they are stressed about how you will respond or react. When you are content or neutral, people are less likely to feel like they are walking on eggshells. People may want to please you because you are their leader; that is about them. But do you make them feel like they *have* to please you by how you behave?

During a recent discussion with a client—I'll call her Sandy—she admitted that her style of leading involved letting people discuss things. She appreciates consensus, and the group is accustomed to this as Sandy's predecessor also used consensus-style leadership. After leading for a couple years, Sandy was struggling in having the group make decisions. Some people would not show up for votes, provided dissenting opinions, and created dissonance within the team. Her vision for the department was stalled, and they were not making progress.

Aside from asking questions of folks and bringing people together, what does Sandy bring to the table? How can she add value to the team? What does the team need to be able to move forward on their initiatives? What does the organization need from her to ensure the future success of the department?

Sandy came up with several ways to use her power as the leader to make a bigger impact. She can ensure that decisions are made in a timely manner and are aligned with the vision for the department and the organization. She can ensure that discussions remain positive and helpful. She can offer suggestions, provide perspectives for consideration, and expand people's thinking on the matter up for discussion. She offers them a vision for the department and the view from the helicopter—she has a bigger view of the organization that she can share with the team. And to ensure that decisions are made in a timely manner, she can make decisions with or without a full consensus.

Sandy later learned that her predecessor had struggled with this group, and this was a deciding factor for moving to another position. Employees expect their leader to be decisive, to acquire input and then set the intention for the group. Consensus leadership might be effective at times and in certain contexts—but certainly not in all situations. It can be inefficient and ineffective. Most situations require other leadership styles or a combination of approaches. What do your employees (or your employer) need from you to move things forward and get things accomplished?

Another client shared the impact his boss had on the leadership team. He stated that this boss distributed the work and led discussions at meetings but never brought anything to the team. She did not share much information, assumed people knew things without sharing important details, and was not clear regarding her strategies. She did not offer assistance or support in accomplishing what was discussed. Although she stated that people could come to her with questions, no one felt comfortable or safe speaking with her, nor did they feel that she could offer them anything.

This boss did not offer to find out information or do any research to bring back to the group. She handed out the work (demonstrating good delegation), but the emphasis was on what everyone else was going to do, never what she could or would do to support the team's efforts. My client shared that it felt as if this executive saw herself as separate and too important to participate in the team. It felt very top-down and matriarchal. She functioned as if her role was to ensure that everyone else did their jobs while she contributed nothing.

Without providing information, perspective, vision, or direction, without clear communication, trust in your team, safety, or support, what are you actually contributing as the leader? You will add value in many different ways. There is an opportunity here to discover what you do that matters to the organization and impacts others, as well as identify ways in which you want to leave your mark.

Create a Healthy Work Environment

A great amount of research has been conducted over decades to discover what makes a work environment healthy and positive, one where people enjoy coming to work and remain employed there, one where people are attracted to work—where there is minimal turnover, and it is easy to recruit when positions are vacant. In fact, the research project for my dissertation focused on the qualities of a healthy work environment and its impact on job satisfaction.

After reading hundreds of research studies, along with conducting my own research on work environment and employee outcomes, I realized the conclusions were quite clear. A healthy work environment is one where collaboration and teamwork are championed, growth and development of the individual is supported, recognition is provided, and employees are involved in decision-making. In a healthy work environment, leaders are authentic, positive, fair, and accessible. People are offered autonomy and empowerment with the support necessary to be successful. There is an appropriate workload and staffing level, skilled and clear communication, and a focus on health and safety at work. We know this to be the case. It's been studied, and the research has been replicated in numerous workplaces and industries. When these factors are present, people report higher self-efficacy, organizational commitment, and job satisfaction. This is not new information.

So why do we struggle to ensure that we provide healthy work environments? First, we need to define what it means to create a work environment.

The work environment is defined by how people feel from their interaction within the workplace. It is created by the interactions of employees, the work, policies, and leaders. It is the space we create within which people come together to perform their work and achieve outcomes and is based on how people feel working in that space. It's how we experience our work together.

An individual interacts within the workplace, and those interactions then influence how the individual behaves in that environment. Reactions to that behavior then determine how the environment supports or encourages continued actions within it. Leadership plays a significant role in how people are expected to behave, what gets rewarded (or not), how people interact or collaborate, and how people are treated at work. The experience people have at work impacts their health and well-being as well as their level of satisfaction.[30]

Satisfaction (or dissatisfaction) is an emotional response to the individual's experience within the environment. Generally, people report satisfaction with mentally challenging and interesting work, positive recognition for performance, feelings of personal accomplishment, and support received from others. As social beings, we create an environment through our interactions among fellow employees and leadership that impacts how we feel about our work and ourselves in relation to our work and the organization.

Several factors contribute to employee health and well-being at work, including both work factors and individual factors. Work factors include work demands, how work is organized, role clarity, meaning of work and how it relates to the organizational mission, possibilities for development opportunities, and ability to use influence, interpersonal relations with leaders, support systems, and a sense of community, feedback, and support. Leaders can impact all these things. Leader support is an important protective factor against a stressful environment.[31]

Personal factors also impact an individual's ability to cope with stressors. These factors include their resilience, how well they manage conflict, whether they ask for help, and the other things that are happening in their lives. Family and support systems outside of work also impact one's ability to cope. Individuals play a role in their own health and well-being and in the impact they have on the work environment as well.

Negative and unhealthy work environments are costly to an organization. Poor working conditions, heavy workloads, lack of support by leadership, and low pay coupled with long hours and lack of recognition can lead to turnover as well as poor morale, low productivity, and increased use of sick time, all of which impact the organization's bottom line.

It pays dividends to do what we can as leaders to promote a positive and healthy work environment, one where people feel cared about and supported, and where people feel a sense of belonging and a greater sense that they are part of a mission that is contributing to the betterment of the world in some (even small) way.

Management strategies can mitigate stress in the workplace, and leaders can focus on keeping people safe, healthy, and satisfied. It is not easy to create these things in practice. It requires intention and attention, a concerted effort to ensure that people's basic needs for safety, security, and belonging are met at work and that there are also opportunities for their higher-level needs for autonomy, development, challenge, and self-actualization to be met.

There are many things in the organization that could be impacted to create a better work environment and a less stressful workplace. Do people have a sense of control? Do they feel supported? Are there a lot of conflicts in the workplace? Is there work overload? Do people have some decision-making authority? How well do people get along? Is teamwork and collaboration encouraged when appropriate? Is the workplace respectful?

The key qualities found in a healthy work environment include acknowledgment and appreciation, involvement in decision-making (autonomy), clear communication, leader authenticity and effectiveness, respectful interactions, opportunities for personal and professional growth, teamwork and collaboration, and trust and safety. Interestingly, none of these are about the work itself but rather what happens at work and how organizations provide a work environment supportive of employees. This requires leaders to have the skills needed to support, encourage, acknowledge, and develop employees, so they can create positive feelings within the work environment that can spread throughout the team. A positive work environment and emphasis on being one's best at work offers people the ability to thrive in the workplace and contribute what is possible.

Control What You Can

> *God, grant me the serenity to accept the things I cannot change, the courage to change the things I can, and the wisdom to know the difference.*

—THE SERENITY PRAYER AS PENNED BY
KARL PAUL REINHOLD NIEBUHR

The Serenity Prayer is routinely stated at the end of Alcoholics Anonymous meetings as a way of teaching people struggling with addiction the importance of surrender and acceptance. Regardless of your faith or religion, regardless of whether you believe in a higher power, the Serenity Prayer is a reminder to let go of those things over which you have no control and to focus on what you can do, what is in your power to do, to make an impact in your world.

It is so easy to get distracted by things over which you have no control, and it is very stressful. You have no control over what people choose to do or say or the requests they make. A huge source of frustration is wishing, hoping, praying, or wanting things (or people) to be different. If you are feeling frustrated, listen to your thoughts around the situation. What do you wish were different?

Frustration often feels like you are walking into a wall and hitting your head. You keep bumping your head into the wall over and over again, wishing and hoping things would change. Perhaps the wall will move out of the way this time.

Surrender means letting go of the hope that the thing, person, or situation will be different than it is. The wall will not budge no matter how hard you push. Surrender is the process of letting go, of no longer trying to force your will onto something you do not control or have power over. Once you let go of continuing to force your will, you experience relief—the freedom from pushing and striving and not getting anywhere. Stress subsides, and you regain your power.

When you let go, you realize you have options. You can turn to the left or to the right, or you can turn around. What are these circumstances asking of you? What might you do to approach this situation, person, or thing to bring about a different result? Clearly, it requires actions other than how you have been approaching it.

The reality is that there is a wall and you have bumped up against it. By acknowledging the problem specifically, you gain the power to choose a different course of action.

There are many examples of how this might show up in your life and work. One client shared how she was so frustrated by her workplace not providing the resources or support she needed. She had spent years trying to get her leaders to change the culture, their methods, and their procedures—to no avail. She contacted me when she had finally given up all hope for things to be different. She realized that in order to find peace and regain her power, she needed to find new employment.

A friend recently shared how frustrated she was with her life situation. Her husband was ill and now she must do more of the work in the relationship (this is the "in sickness" part of marriage). In the conversation, it was clear that although she was doing what needed to be done, she was unhappy about it. She struggled because she wished her reality were different (that her husband was healthy), to the point where she was harboring negativity over the situation. Her power was in her ability to choose her attitude and approach to how her life events were unfolding.

Wishing someone would do something faster or differently at work, wishing others would not ask you for certain things, hoping things will improve when you do not have the ability to bring about the changes needed—these are all examples of areas of frustration and a loss of agency. As the saying goes, hope is not a strategy. If you are frustrated, reflect on the situation: what is the person doing, how would you like it to be different, what have you done to correct it, and what might you be missing? What might you need to accept so you can approach this situation or person differently?

Often leaders will tell me they are frustrated by someone's behavior at work. What have they done to correct the problem? Have they discussed it with that individual? Sometimes they have not addressed it directly; other times they have but nothing has changed. There is a message in the individual's behavior. If your instructions have been crystal clear and the individual is not doing what needs to be done, then they don't understand, don't care, or can't do it. What needs to happen now? Facing reality means acknowledging what is, not wishing it were different. Avoiding issues will not make change happen. Silence gives the behavior permission. You cannot control others, but you can provide direction and clarity around expectations, and you can offer assistance and support. And if that does not work, then perhaps the job is not the best fit for that person.

You control you—your thoughts, emotions, and actions—what I refer to as TEA. You control your thoughts when you notice them—

you may not control the first thought, but you can control the thoughts that follow. Mindfulness means paying attention to the thoughts in your head. When you notice yourself overthinking, getting lost in a story you are making up, or catastrophizing, you have the power to catch yourself and stop. Just stop. Choose to think differently, find a distraction, strike up a conversation with someone about something else entirely, or ask someone to help you think through the problem. Do not stay in your own head ruminating or creating stories. Focus on a more pleasant and effective action.

Some people enjoy thinking about their problems because this is how they self-soothe. They find comfort in being able to assess and analyze their situation. While this is certainly helpful, we have already learned that it can be a tough place to remain for long by yourself. We need each other to validate our thoughts, question our ideas, and gain perspective and different viewpoints.

Emotions are inner messages. They are another way we obtain information about what is happening in our surroundings. Noticing and naming what you are feeling helps you gain power to use the information to act. While you cannot stop emotions from rising up within you, you can notice them and ask questions about their arrival. Sadness cues you to the fact that something is lost; anger lets you know that something is not right, and a boundary has been crossed; joy helps you feel deeply that which is beautiful or awesome. Stopping to assess what is happening will help you access power over your responses.

Paying attention to your thoughts and feelings—being mindful—requires awareness and focus. When we are so busy or so transactional, we forget that being human means we have feelings, spirits, and bodies as well as minds. Our bodies need rest and time to rejuvenate, as well as movement, good nutrition, and adequate sleep. Our minds also need time to disconnect and recharge. Our spirits need tending and care to be able to connect to the world, to others, and to ourselves. Our spirit connects us to universal wisdom and is how we access our intuition. Each realm—physical, emotional, spiritual, and mental—requires our attention and care. Focusing on ourselves in these areas enables us to be more fully present, more self-aware, and more in control of our actions, especially when we are triggered by some situation or someone's behavior.

When we are faced with things beyond our control at work, we can acknowledge them, which helps us connect with others and resonate with them. The pandemic taught us so much about ourselves and how we are all connected in so many ways. What impacts one can have rippling effects on the world.

Stressors occurring in the world or in our local communities may or may not directly affect people with whom we work, yet they can certainly have an impact on us. These include political instability, economic uncertainty, climate change, volatility, uncertainty, and violence, among others. We often have no control over these events, but we may feel something when they occur. We do control how we address them at work or whether we at least recognize that people may be impacted by things beyond the workplace.

While often not discussed openly in the workplace, community or world events cause stress. Often people keep their heads down and focus on the task at hand. It can be so overwhelming, where you feel so powerless that you do not consider how these events impact you or your employees emotionally. Just being aware of what may be occurring in people's lives and in the world at large can help you connect with others and create safety for them to experience whatever they are experiencing. What you can do is start with yourself, noting how the events are impacting you, and then pay attention to how they might be impacting others.

What might you be carrying that may be impacting you and your level of stress? Do not minimize. If you are feeling something and it is impacting you, it could affect how you show up. Look for the impact a community event or worldwide situation may be having on others. If others are impacted, that could affect their work as well.

Focus on what you can do: you can be present, care about how others may be feeling, ask how others are doing, and pay attention to behavior changes. Sharing your own thoughts, ideas, fears, and feelings can be therapeutic and demonstrates vulnerability, which opens the door for others to feel more comfortable sharing what is happening to them.

In Part III, we turn our attention to another core activity of leadership: connecting.

PART III

CARE to Connect

> *Only by working harmoniously in*
> *co-operation with other individuals or*
> *groups of individuals and thus creating*
> *value and benefit for them, will one create*
> *sustainable achievement for oneself.*
>
> —NAPOLEON HILL

In Part II, we explored many ways to advance your leadership by identifying the stressors you face and their impact on you and your leadership. We acknowledged how organizational stressors also play a role in employee outcomes such as satisfaction and engagement. We learned that we could reduce friction to make it easier for people to do their best work and elicit, encourage, and inspire people to perform at their best. We also learned to pay attention to how we add value and how our presence and actions create a work environment where people can thrive.

In Part III, we explore the other major activity of leadership: connection. Leadership is about relationships. We manage tasks and we lead people. To build relationships, we must care. C-A-R-E provides an acronym for what leaders can do for and with employees and others to connect, build trust, and demonstrate compassion for people at work. CARE stands for communicate, appreciate, respect, and empathize.

As Theodore Roosevelt said, "Nobody cares how much you know until they know how much you care."

CHAPTER 7

Communicate Effectively

> *The art of communication is the*
> *language of leadership.*
>
> —JAMES HUMES

C ommunicating is connecting. With each encounter, each conversation, you have the opportunity to connect with people, to understand them, to share yourself with them, and to be understood. Your presence itself makes a statement. Your mannerisms and how you show up tells people how to treat you and sends messages about how you feel about yourself and how you expect others to behave in your presence. Effective communication is one of the most important tasks of a leader to connect with others at all levels.

When leaders fail to communicate effectively, people are not clear about what they need to do, and the uncertainty increases stress levels as people try to do the best they can yet live in fear of not performing well. Failures in communication abound—from conflict, misunderstandings, and lack of clarity to even what is left unsaid. To be good leaders, we must learn ways to communicate more effectively, address challenges and conflicts when they emerge, and continue to practice ways to be clearer in our communications.

What is effective communication? How will you know that you are communicating well and that what you are communicating is enough? And what should you be communicating? Although we are constantly communicating, there is an art to it, and we must develop our skills in saying what needs to be said, using nonverbals effectively, and practicing active listening.

Can you ever overcommunicate? If you are repeating information or providing too much detail or more information than is necessary to make your point, then yes, you can overcommunicate. However, people need to hear things several times in several different ways in order for the ideas to sink in. In a hybrid workforce, it is hard to know whether people are receiving timely information. Overcommunicating, or repeating information, can be helpful to ensure people understand the information and to clear up any misconceptions.

Withholding information can be detrimental and can also represent power hoarding. Trusting your employees with information is important. It is part of building a relationship with your staff. In his book, *The Thin Book of Trust*, Charles Feltman described the four attributes of trust as care, sincerity, reliability, and competence.[32] Feltman declared that of these attributes, care is the most important. For your people to trust you, they need to know you care about them.

While there is much involved in communication that is beyond the scope of this book, in this chapter we explore those things leaders do to communicate effectively. These include clearly communicating vision and values, expectations, requests, and boundaries, known as V-E-R-B.

Communicate a Compelling Vision

Leadership is the capacity to translate a vision into reality.

—Warren Bennis

When I was a young business student at Temple University, the professor likened leadership to corralling a school of fish. At first, everyone is swimming in different directions doing their own thing. The leader's job is to get everyone swimming in the same direction and moving toward a common goal or outcome (Figure 2).

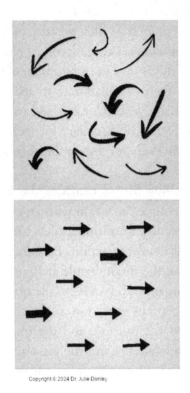

Figure 2. Moving in the same direction: The result from a compelling vision.

Leaders provide a trajectory using a vision to set the course. A compelling vision informs people of the direction for the company, department, or group. As the captain of the ship, the leader must inform people of the destination so that they can focus on achieving that outcome. In a famous example, President John F. Kennedy envisioned that the United States would reach the moon by the end of the decade (1970) and made that part of his strategy for his presidency. That vision began the process of developing the national space exploration program.

Vision communicates direction to the team, group, or organization. Without vision, people do what they can with what they know and mostly focus on their own work. They each swim in the direction that best suits the individual.

With vision, people start the process of swimming together toward a common outcome. People have a better understanding of how each person's work fits into the attainment of what is possible and are therefore better suited to collaborate to achieve results. Vision is that point on the horizon we can look at and work toward achieving. While each of us performs the necessary job duties to ensure the ship is running properly, we keep our eye on the horizon, so we do not lose our course.

While a compelling vision provides the beacon and sets the course, leaders must couple the vision with an explanation of why we are headed in that direction. Inspiring leaders have a clear purpose and rationale behind their course of action. President Kennedy explained that putting people on the moon would help us gain knowledge and understanding for humankind. Not everyone agreed with his rationale that this was an appropriate direction at the time. However, people needed to understand the purpose and the importance of traveling this path. When people understand the reasoning behind the vision, they can get excited about jumping on board and becoming involved in making the vision come to life. People get inspired by a clear and compelling vision and become motivated to do their part in creating a successful product, service, or outcome, like landing on the moon.

In his popular TED Talk, Simon Sinek discussed the importance of starting with understanding why you do what you do.[33] Sinek stated that "people don't buy what you do; they buy why you do it." This extends to employees as well as customers. Vision and purpose engage and inspire people. This is necessary for people to align with what you believe is possible so that they, too, can believe in it, work toward achieving it, and stay the course.

When I started as the director of nursing, I needed to paint a picture for my team of where we were headed. Some of my nurses were really unhappy with the state of the department and were already looking for new jobs. Their complaints included the lack of support by leadership, the lack of empowerment, and the mistreatment of nursing staff by others. They felt very disrespected and taken advantage of in many ways. After listening to their complaints, assessing the needs of the department, and considering what I felt was important for the department, I shared a vision with my staff charting a course for our future.

Understanding their issues was important because change was not going to happen overnight; it would take some time to make the changes needed to get where we were going. And people needed to get on board. I needed people to believe that change was possible, that the vision I articulated was where nursing should be and what it should look like in this setting, and they needed to see how their values and desires fit into the vision and what we would be creating.

One nurse in particular was exceptionally bright, very knowledgeable, personable, and well-liked—a natural leader. People looked up to her. However, she had been unhappy in her current role and with her schedule, felt mistreated by the previous leader, and was actively seeking new employment. I learned of her impending departure through meetings with several of the other nursing staff. They did not want her to leave.

While this nurse did not have an official title, clearly, she was the unofficial leader of the nursing staff. They appreciated her presence and depended on her. She had a significant impact on the success and quality of the nursing care provided, and she needed to stay.

I met with her individually and asked her what challenges she was facing, what she wanted, and what was important to her. We did not know each other well—I had only been there a couple of months. I had not developed much trust with anyone yet, but I knew we needed her to stay. I also knew she did not really want to leave; she loved working there with the children. In my vision, I saw her being an integral part of our success. I shared my vision for the future with her. I also shared what I wanted her role to be to help make this vision a reality. I was very honest with her—regardless of what had transpired in the past, we were headed in a new direction, and she would play a key role in helping us achieve the success desired. I needed to convey this to her in a way that would get her to reconsider.

She did reconsider and remained with us. This nurse went on to play a vital role in creating the change in culture and work environment we intended. She was instrumental in the success we experienced during my tenure in that leadership role. We were able to make some quick changes to reduce the personal challenges and stressors she faced at work and alter her responsibilities, which made it easier and more enjoyable for her to stay with us and to thrive.

Communicate Your Values

While vision provides the beacon or the destination, values provide the guidelines for how we will work together to achieve that vision. Values are the guiding principles that provide standards for behavior. Values speak to what is important and inform your decisions daily.

Most companies have stated values. Their values reflect what is important to that company and how they expect people to behave. Some companies also have leadership principles, which delineate how the company expects its leaders to behave. Amazon's leadership principles, for example, include thinking big to serve customers in new ways, having a bias for action to move things along quickly, and ownership, meaning they expect people to work on behalf of the entire company, not just their own area.[34]

How the leaders of a company live their stated values and bring them to life forwards the agenda of the business entity and creates the intended culture. You are responsible for upholding the values of the organization as well as any values that are important to you and to your leadership agenda. Knowing what values matter most to you is an exercise well worth the time and effort to explore so that you are intentional about how you show up and how you lead others.

You are in the spotlight and now have the opportunity to chart a course for yourself and others that can improve things in your organization and in your part of the world to make it a better place to work and live. There is power in your position; it's time to use the power wisely.

At the start of my leadership role, to help my staff understand me, what I stood for, and what to expect from me as a leader, I revealed my values and explained what each value meant to me and why it was important. My guiding principles included integrity, respect, excellence, and fun. These are the things I value most, and they instruct how I live my life. They became important guiding principles in my leadership activities as well.

Integrity meant that we were always going to do the right thing given what the situation warranted. There were going to be situations that did not have a clear response and required discussion to determine the appropriate course of action. Ethical situations often have many possible perspectives. In those instances, we would talk candidly to figure out what our best strategy might be, but we would never compromise our integrity. Making this a priority opened the door to frank discussions and listening to one another's perspectives. Everyone had a voice to contribute to the conversation.

In nursing school, we learned the importance of respecting our licenses. It was an honor and a privilege—and a lot of hard work—to earn that credential. If we were not careful, then it could be revoked. We also took an oath to do good and to do no harm. Ethics is a large part of nursing work, and ethical issues abound. There are times when the right thing to do is not the popular thing, the least expensive thing, or the most convenient one. Yet when you stand for integrity, you do what is right, even when no one is watching and the only person it impacts is you. You know when you do not do the right thing, and that impacts how you show up.

Another stated value was that we were always going to treat each other with respect and kindness. This was nonnegotiable. Because this was so clear, it was easy for me to address bad behavior and poor performance when they occurred. We had enough challenges with the patients (and their families); there was no way we would tolerate inappropriate behavior from other professionals.

The value of respect guided how we treated agency staff, new hires, other departments—everyone. Bad behavior, poor work quality, and any form of disrespect or bullying would not be tolerated. This included how the nurses were treated. We would not tolerate being treated with disrespect as had been experienced by nurses previously. Respect was also important to the organization and was identified in the handbook under their list of values, making it an easy standard to follow. I just needed to uphold it.

One way I upheld this value for my team was when they encountered particularly difficult family members, challenging interactions with other staff, or difficulty with doctors. I would step in to help with any situation that was taking up time and energy beyond the normal scope of practice. There were times when a nurse was dealing with a parent who was screaming or cursing and was unable to calm them. Given the work they already had to manage, I would handle the parent. This was one way I could provide assistance and support and reduce friction. If the nurse could not get what he or she needed from a physician—perhaps they were unavailable—the nurse would contact me, and I would be sure they got their needs met in order to provide quality care for the children, whether that meant contacting other doctors or calling 911. We would determine the best course of action for the patient, and I would do what I could to provide that assistance.

When you are clear about your standards and stand up for your values and the respectful treatment of others, you become someone whom others want to emulate. Your standards become those that others aspire to, and in this way, you change the world. It starts with you and how you show up. You impact those around you and those with whom you interact. They adopt the standards and values and share them with others—their family, friends, and community. It spreads outward and creates ripples as you devise a path and chart a course for others to follow. High standards enable others to rise together.

Our value of excellence meant we would strive for continuous improvement. In nursing, as in many professions, there are often changes in regulations and best practices. We would remain vigilant, ask questions, look for inefficiencies in how we provided care, and seek ways to improve our procedures and processes. This kept people open to possibilities for innovation and creativity at work. We were always looking for ways to improve things.

Fun was an important value for several reasons. Perhaps *fun* is not the best word to describe this value, but it was important to me that we enjoyed our work as much as possible. Work can be stressful! And we do things to ourselves that make our lives harder; we can be so serious, focused, and intense that we lose perspective. Some people are perfectionistic and beat themselves up when things do not go as planned or as they intended. It is important to keep things in perspective and to lighten up when possible. This is another polarity where we must balance being serious and focused with being lighthearted and joyful. Without the lightness of fun, we can forget to enjoy ourselves and the work we are doing. For me, this was important to remember.

Although I shared these important guiding principles with my staff, talk is meaningless without action behind the words. I needed to live these values daily and teach others how to live them as well, through both action and word. Being your word and doing as you say you will do is an important quality of leadership and one of Don Miguel Ruiz's four agreements, which is a powerful code of personal conduct.[35] These values gave my team standards for how they would operate, making things easier and less stressful because they knew what to expect and how to behave. They were clear about what standards we were following, so there would be no surprises.

What is your vision for success? What would you like to see your department, team, or group deliver? How do you see them functioning and working together? How will it feel to work there? What are you hoping to achieve, and why is that important? What do you believe about this vision for success?

What are your guiding principles? What are the values you want your department, team, or group to use to navigate the workplace?

Why are these important to you, and what is important about them for your team? What will they give you or provide for you and others? How will you operationalize them or use them in actions or behaviors? How will this make decision-making easier?

Communicate Clear Expectations

If you don't know where you are going, how will you know when you've arrived?

Clear communication is critical for successful leadership. Clarity around vision (where are we headed?) and values (what is important?) is a wonderful place to start. Another key component of effective communication is providing clear expectations—for the work, for deliverables, for timelines, and for behavior. Setting clear expectations answers the question "What should I be doing?" Effectively communicating expectations defines what people should be doing, when, and with whom. It is important to be as clear as possible, so there are no questions about how people should behave or what they should do when and how much.

People need clarity; they need to know what is expected of them if they are to perform well and provide optimal output. They need standards for how they are expected to behave and clarity around what behaviors will—or will not—be tolerated. People do not know unless expectations are explicitly communicated. Otherwise, people will guess, and let's face it, people are not good at guessing.

Be clear about your expectations. Often leaders do not spend enough time clarifying what they want. I have met with many leaders interested in hiring someone to fill a position, but they had not yet considered what qualities they desired in the ideal candidate. They knew what they wanted the new hire to do but had not identified the qualities that would be important to succeed at that work and fit into the culture. You must know what you want, so you can assess the person based on those qualities.

Then you need to communicate those expectations clearly to others. People are not mind readers, so it is important we do not leave our instructions open for interpretation. Often, however, leaders make assumptions about what people know or do not know. Leaders may assume something is common knowledge, but it could be known only to that leader given their education and experience. Or there may be unwritten rules that someone made up long ago, rules that may not support success today. You must define success and then communicate specifically what that would look like.

One way to ensure that everyone is on the same page is to create a team charter, rules of conduct, or mutual agreements—whatever you want to call them. Leaders will often bring in a team coach to facilitate discussions with the team to identify what is important in how people treat one another, how conflicts will be managed, and the overall behaviors expected in working together. This is where you take all those unwritten rules about "how things are done around here" and make them explicit. This enables you to identify clear rules for engagement where everyone knows what is expected. It is important to hold people accountable to these standards. This way, even new hires know exactly what to expect and how to behave. It is a way of acculturating people to the norms of the department or group.

In the movie *Philadelphia*, Denzel Washington plays a lawyer. Several times in the movie, his character says, "Tell it to me like I'm a six-year-old." This has stuck with me over the years and reminds me that people have various levels of education and ability for understanding. People also have difficulty putting their thoughts into words and often struggle to explain themselves.

During the process of completing my doctoral dissertation, I had to write an informed consent form for people to sign in order to participate in my research project. To ensure that people could understand exactly what was expected of them and what rights they had when participating as a research subject, the consent form had to be written at an eighth grade reading level. This was so difficult that it took me at least forty hours to whittle down the language to meet the requirements. We must be really careful and clear with our intentions and language if we want others to fully comprehend our meaning.

Asking people to summarize what has been said, or what they heard you say, is an effective way to ensure that you are both understanding things the same way. One of my nurses had a way of hearing things I did not say nor mean. In fact, when I would ask her, "Tell me what you heard me say," she would reply with something entirely different. I quickly realized that I needed to have a third party present for our discussions (usually someone from human resources, but sometimes it had to be another member of my nursing leadership team) since she seemed to hear things as she wanted to hear them and not as they were actually communicated to her. Perhaps it was my communication style, or perhaps it was how she interpreted what I said. Regardless, it was important that we understood one another clearly.

Remember playing "whisper down the lane" as a child, where the first person in line tells a story, and that story then gets passed to the next person and then the next? Remember how the story would get completely muddled and changed by the time it reached the last person in line? Stories have a way of being elaborated upon and embellished or diminished with critical information missing. The meaning of the story can be completely altered by the time some people hear it. This is why people need to hear the information from leadership, repeated frequently, completely, and even written down, so they can read it for themselves and learn the exact details without someone else interpreting it. Adults learn through repetition and in different ways such as verbal, written, and demonstration.

Do not assume anything. The brain makes assumptions naturally—this is how it synthesizes information. When it comes to other people and what they are thinking or what they know, you have to check those assumptions to ensure they are accurate. Our assumptions are often incorrect. Clarify or validate your assumptions. That will save time and the need to mend the relationship after arguing because of misguided assumptions.

Make things crystal clear, specific, concise, and not up for interpretation. Eliminate fancy words or terminology. Do not use acronyms unless you are completely sure everyone knows what they mean.

Sometimes in our team meetings, the clinical staff would rattle off acronyms that the rest of the team did not know or understand. This meant having to stop the meeting to ask them to explain themselves, which took time and detracted from the essence of the meeting. Don't make assumptions about what people know and what they do not know. If you make an assumption, then ask the person if they are familiar with what you are presenting so that you can be sure you are both clearly understanding what is being discussed.

Many misunderstandings are born from not seeing or interpreting things in the same way. Your goal is to avoid such misunderstandings as much as possible. Think of it this way—people's knowledge about something can be seen as being on a continuum. Your knowledge and understanding are also on a continuum. As the speaker, you have information you want to share. How do you know where your listeners are on that continuum? Assessing that first helps you save time by allowing you to meet them where they are. It is possible that when you ask them about their understanding of something, they know what you know. Then you can discuss the topic without describing it in detail or telling them something they already know.

Meeting others where they are on the continuum helps you build trust; it demonstrates respect for where they are, and it helps you assess how much you will need to share with them—and how much might be too much. Meet them where they are and bring them along that continuum a little at a time, so they can grow at their own pace. You cannot expect others to meet you where you are as you are further along on the continuum. Many people get frustrated with other people's behaviors. If you catch yourself thinking, "They should know better" or "They should know that," stop and take a step back to consider what that behavior or performance might be communicating to you. If they did really know, they would behave differently. "If they knew better, they would do better." Their behavior is telling you that they really do not know the expectations or may not have the knowledge needed to perform that task correctly. Ask them what they are thinking and what they think is expected.

Disappointment relates directly to unmet expectations. What were you expecting, and was that aligned with the information the other person expected? The first step is to understand whether you were both thinking the same way. By leaning in and being curious about what they know, you can learn so much about where the person is and their training or knowledge level. Too often, we get angry, assume the person should know, conclude they just aren't behaving or performing as they should, and jump right to disciplining them.

Instead, give the person (initially) the benefit of the doubt by assuming that you missed something in your instruction or expectations. Explore whether that person has the information needed to perform as expected. In doing so, you take responsibility to assess what they know or don't know. This makes them feel that you care about their work or behavior and that perhaps you failed them in some way if they are underperforming. It lets the person off the hook for the moment, gives permission for the lapse in behavior, and affords the individual an excuse and an opportunity to be wrong without "getting in trouble." The opportunity exists for both parties to be honest without judgment. This clears the space for a conversation where you clarify expectations and provide essential information or even training to ensure the person is set up for success and is clear about what is expected. You cannot hold people to a standard that is not clear or that they do not understand and expect them to do good work.

Once you have that conversation, you can document it, and then if the problem persists or if the person is not following directions or meeting expectations, you can try something different or assess their fit in the role. You may need to start the discipline process, but not until you are sure that you have done everything you can do to help them succeed. If they cannot rise to the occasion, then it might be time to have a frank discussion about whether this job is a good match for their strengths and skills and what kind of work they really want to be doing.

Ambiguity is stressful. Lack of clear communication from managers is one of the main reasons people leave their jobs. There has been a lot of research conducted on role clarity and the need for clear communication from leaders. Being held to standards that are not explicit sets people up to fail. People also cannot live up to unrealistic or unreasonable expectations.

Unmanageable workload or demands or unreasonable time pressure creates unnecessary stress. Pay attention to what you expect of others and how people respond to the standards you set for your employees. Create a work environment that supports open and candid conversations, so you can have conversations with your employees about the challenges they are facing on the job.

Communicate Your Requests

Direct communication includes clarity when making requests. Making requests is asking for what you need. It answers the questions: "What do I need? What does our team need? Who can help get this accomplished?" This means knowing specifically what you want or need help with and then asking for that support.

We all have needs—personal needs, emotional needs, and needs for assistance. It's part of being human and navigating through our activities. Personal needs include needs for attention and autonomy, for humor and play, and for meaning and connection. We also have needs for physical well-being, safety, and security. At work we have a need to collaborate, to work as a team, to be recognized, to be heard and seen, and to be appreciated. We have a lot of needs.

Most of us do not realize our needs. We tend to be out of touch with what is really going on within our bodies and minds. Why is that? Because we avoid our feelings. Feelings bring our attention to something we are experiencing. As I have mentioned, feelings are our inner messaging system. Most of us are not taught how to use that messaging system. Underneath our feelings is an unmet need.

Feelings are often misunderstood. When we are overwhelmed, for example, that typically means we are trying to do too much. Are we putting too much pressure on ourselves to perform in a certain way? Are we taking on too much without adequate time to address the task or project? Are we not asking others for support or to share in the workload? What might be the underlying need you have for taking on so much work? What might you need to do to care for or respect yourself differently? The antidote for overwhelm is to simplify. What thoughts, feelings, or fears come up for you when you think about simplifying your workload? In what ways might you need to delegate, prioritize, put some things off, or let some things go? Notice any resistance you may have.

We get angry when people do not do as we had expected or hoped. What is the underlying need? We needed something to get done, or we needed to be treated in a certain way. People do the best they know how to do. So, this implores us to consider some questions: Have we made sure that person knows what they should be doing (i.e., have we made the performance expectations clear)? Have we made sure the person understands how we want to be treated or how to behave in our team?

Take the time to consider whether your language was clear and direct or whether there was room for interpretation and misunderstanding. Our requests are often muddled. If you take ownership first, then you can decide how to explain what you need from that individual. You can also inquire as to what they think they should be doing. This provides you with information about what they know and what they do not know. We can assume they should know something, but assumptions are not truths and can cause friction and misunderstandings.

People often assume that others know what they want or need. If you hear yourself think, "They should know to do that," but they are not doing what you intended, then their behavior is telling you that the instructions are not clear, and they do not know what you want.

We make a lot of assumptions. And while this is how the mind makes sense of things, as Don Miguel Ruiz reminds us in his book

The Four Agreements, the problem is that we believe our assumptions are truth, which they are not.[36] (The third of the four agreements is "Don't Make Assumptions.")

We make assumptions about what others are doing or thinking. We assume others think and feel the way we do. We assume things about ourselves as well, not being honest about what we want or need, what we can or cannot do, and we often overestimate or underestimate our abilities. Without inquiry or clarification, we assume our thoughts are true, and we draw conclusions based on our faulty thinking.

When we do this, we can become emotionally attached to these ideas, and then, when reality does not match our thoughts about how things should be, that creates discord. We can become angry or resentful. All this takes place in our minds. If the incongruence between our thoughts and reality occurs due to someone else, we take that personally and become angry and defensive. Although it's not about us, we make it about us.

When you notice that you feel something about how someone is behaving or performing, stop and assess what that means for you. What are you feeling specifically? What is the need you have that might be unmet? Only once you have identified your underlying need can you then determine how you want to approach the person so that you can express your feelings, clarify your needs, and make your request known.

In his book *Nonviolent Communication*, Dr. Marshall Rosenberg teaches that requests should be made in clear, positive, and action language.[37] Say what you need to say, make your request, and then have the other person reflect back what they heard you say. This gives you the opportunity to correct their understanding and clarify if needed and ensures that your request is understood in the way you intended.

Rosenberg also shares that requests can be received as demands if the person can expect consequences for noncompliance. We want people to comply willingly with our requests. Ultimately, as leaders, we want to tap into people's sense of responsibility, desire to do the right thing, and longing to be their best.

People want to do a good job. They want to be great employees, great friends, and great spouses. Most of the time, people really just don't know how to behave differently. It's your job to teach them by communicating directly—identify what you want, don't assume others think the same way as you or know what you're thinking, speak your truth simply and clearly, and do so without any emotional charge. People are more productive, happier, and experience deeper, healthier, and more meaningful relationships when each party is willing and able to speak their truth directly. As you become more adept at this, you may need to teach others how to speak their truth as well. Don't assume they know how.

There will be situations when, as a leader, you must enforce boundaries or expectations with discipline or a more direct and clear-cut statement. Sometimes people do not understand the request, and sometimes people are not interested in following your lead. They may be attached to their own ideas about how things should be done.

Requests are important to ensure clarity, debunk any misconceptions, and ensure that the unspoken is articulated and known. The clearer we are about what we want or need, the easier it will be for the person to accept the request and complete it. If *you* don't know what you want, how can you expect others to know? Stop and consider what it is you want from this person or what needs to be done. The clearer you are about your vision for success, the easier it will be to share it with others.

In addition to personal needs, we also have needs for support in getting the work accomplished. This is where we delegate the work and ensure we are utilizing the skills of the people around us wisely.

We never want to assume others know what we are thinking. They are not mind readers. We also do not want to assume we know what others are thinking. We must ask and verify.

When advocating for something at work, we may need to use requests in a different way. Sometimes, to get your needs met, you must find ways to "plant seeds." This is where you mention something you need and provide some ideas about it but don't make a clear request just yet. In this way, you sprinkle the idea of this request to give the other person the opportunity to consider what that will mean for them given the context. Eventually, you will need to make your request clear. You may need to provide a written proposal, including data for what you are requesting. When you do, however, if you have planted seeds, then this will come as no surprise and may even be welcomed since it has been talked about for a while—they have been waiting for the request!

Learning to be direct and specific in your requests takes practice. It requires that you clarify what you want, identify and explore your feelings, and investigate the underlying needs. Then you can make your request simply and confidently without emotional overtones. Once the person reflects back your request and you are both on the same page, you will know there is clarity in communication.

Communicate Your Boundaries

Between stimulus and response, there
is a space. In that space is our power
to choose our response. In our response
lies our growth and our freedom.

—Viktor Frankl

While making requests is about asking for what you need, boundaries let people know what not to do, what does not work, and what is not acceptable. Boundaries are about what you say no to. Although boundaries are important, when communicating a boundary by telling people what does not work, you also will need to ensure that the person knows what to do instead. That is when you might make some requests.

When working in a psychiatric environment, you must be alert, expect the unexpected, and be clear about what is acceptable and what is not. Patients may say totally inappropriate things to you, and you have to be willing to respond appropriately. Even other employees can behave in ways that are not professional at times. As a young person working in this environment, I learned quite quickly that I needed to speak up carefully and respectfully, yet directly. There can be no wishy-washy or unclear language. I had to be clear and concise, so there was no doubt what was appropriate and acceptable and what was not.

Boundaries are the limits you set for yourself and your team for how others may act or speak. They are the lines you draw regarding people's behavior, and they define you. They are not walls to shut people out, but rather limits that keep the unwanted behaviors of others from entering your space. Boundaries are essential for personal health and for creating a healthy work environment. They function as filters, permitting what's acceptable into your life and keeping other elements out. Your boundaries are about what others may do or say to you. Boundaries speak volumes about who you are and what you stand for regarding how people behave in your presence and how they treat you.

Whatever offenders do, you must remember that it's not personal; it's not about you even though it feels personal. Another person's behavior is always about that person and the thoughts they harbor in their mind. For example, if someone raises his voice, swears, or speaks down to you, he may want power; he may need to be heard; he may want attention—whatever the need, it's about him. How he speaks to you is not about you. It is about how he feels about himself. Most of the time, people are oblivious of the impact they have on others. What is important is that you manage your emotions and respond in a way that represents who you are and how you want to be known and teaches him how you expect to be treated.

When someone speaks to you (or around you) in a way that feels unpleasant, the first step is to notice how you feel. Your feelings are your inner messengers, your inner guidance system. When a boundary is crossed, there is a definite physiological response. If someone's comments or actions make you uncomfortable, notice your feelings and any sensations in your body. Note what the person is doing or saying that is evoking in you this reaction and empower yourself by responding appropriately. Often the words in your mind will be something like "This does not work for me." That is a clue that someone has trespassed.

If you can pause when you feel your body respond and take some time to consider what you are feeling, what you are needing, and what you are wanting, then you can learn ways to address these boundary violations. If you cannot do this in the moment, then ask for some time and return to the conversation later once you have assessed your feelings and calmed your emotional state.

If you do not pause, you may react in ways that are not professional or not representative of how you want others to experience you. And when you react in unprofessional or inappropriate ways, you then have to backtrack later to mend the relationship. This can impact your reputation as you become known as someone who is emotionally reactive and unable to remain calm. Then, you have become *that* person, that leader who makes it unsafe for people to share information, where others feel uncomfortable, walk on eggshells, and shrink or fear approaching you with anything.

There will be times when the unexpected happens, when people you think would never behave badly suddenly do something unprofessional, or when colleagues or other professionals behave in ways that are unacceptable. What will you do? How will you handle that? Knowing who you are and standing firmly in your values and ethical standards will help guide your response in such situations.

In nursing school, we learned the importance of being morally responsible. Nursing has a potent code of ethics that is drilled into you during your studies. Licenses are a privilege, not an automatic achievement. You have to earn that credential, and it can be revoked if you do something that goes against our professional code of conduct.

When I started practicing nursing, I followed the professional code of conduct as described by the nursing standards. Over the years it became clear that mistakes occurred because someone deviated from the basics of either nursing practice or good psychiatric practice. I did my best to perform what was expected and follow what I was taught. People may not have always liked that; sometimes people like to take shortcuts. But I respected the rules—they were there for a reason, to keep us safe. If something was not right, I said something. I was unwilling to accept unethical or bad conduct. It just made things easier for me to do the right thing all the time. Like it or not, people knew what to expect while working with me.

One time, I was pulled from one unit to another during the middle of a shift. A nurse became ill and had to leave suddenly. When I arrived, I asked what was needed of me. The medication nurse requested that I give out the medications she had prepared, and she would be in charge and lead the unit. This made sense since she had been there all evening and I had just arrived.

However, when I went into the medication room, all the medications were poured into little cups and signed out as administered. This meant that although she had not yet administered any medications, she had documented them as already given. This is a big no-no in nursing. You do not pour and prepare your medications, and you do not sign them out as given until you have administered them. I did not know what all the pills were just by looking in the cups, and for all I knew, she had already given everyone their medications since they were signed out as given.

I refused and respectfully told her that since the medications were in that state and already signed out as given, she would need to handle them. While she was angry at first, she had no choice but to accept my boundary. There was plenty of other work to be done, and I focused on that work to support the team and provide care for the patients.

It is not always easy to stand up for what you believe is right. It takes courage and a clear sense of your values and integrity. Knowing who you are and what you stand for is part of being a leader. People won't always behave well. You control how you behave.

There was another time as a young nurse when an admissions clerk called and told me I was to accept a patient to my unit and place him directly into locked seclusion. I unequivocally told him absolutely not, that it was illegal to do what was being asked, and honestly, I don't take orders from admissions clerks—only physicians have that authority (although in this case, it would not have mattered). I had to stop them from bringing the patient onto the unit. The clerk was not happy about it, but I was in charge of the unit and stood up for what was right.

Of course, these examples are sensational. Psychiatric hospitals have a lot of extraordinary occurrences. These examples tested me and groomed me to become the leader I am today. Disagreements and ethical challenges stretch you to become more of who you want to become.

One of my nurses was working full time elsewhere and part time for me. He shared with me that one of the nurses he worked with at his other job was often abrupt with the patients. He did not like how she spoke with them. He felt uncomfortable, yet he was uneasy speaking to her about it.

Advocating for the patients is part of our work as nurses. I asked him what was important to him about this. He did not feel her behavior was respectful. So, what was the problem for him about speaking up? Whether it was about being liked or fear that caused him to remain silent, what mattered was what he felt was appropriate and respectful behavior and who he wanted to be as a nurse and patient advocate. He controlled himself. If this was bothering him, then he had a responsibility to do something—either speak to her directly or report the behavior to a supervisor, even if that meant she would get angry at him.

We always do the right thing, even when it is unpopular. We are there to provide the best possible care to the patients, not to appease someone who has seniority (or whatever the case may be—that is just an excuse). Boundaries, advocacy, and speaking up require courage and boldness. It was up to him to define who he wanted to be and what he valued, and then he needed to take a stand for those values.

Once you are clear about your boundaries, educate people as to how to act in your presence. If you never tell anyone how to treat you, they will treat you in whatever way they choose. When you say nothing, you give your power away. You dishonor yourself when you allow others to mistreat you.

If the behavior happens in your department, how you handle it demonstrates to everyone what you expect as far as behavior is concerned. Behavior speaks volumes. If you do nothing, the behavior will occur again. Silence gives the behavior permission.

Being a leader means demanding excellence of others—asking for and expecting others to do and to be their best. When they miss the mark, bring it to their attention. Do not tolerate less than their best. When you assert yourself and point out inappropriate behavior, you demonstrate leadership, exhibit self-respect, and become a role model for others.

Asserting boundaries requires some key skills. The first is clarity for how people are expected to treat one another. A breach in those expectations requires you to muster your courage and boldly speak up to address the behavior. Effective leaders understand that people will behave in unexpected ways. People will be in bad moods and can be snarky at times. Personalities will clash. People may not like some of the folks they work with. Leaders hold the space for people to be great, knowing that people do not always know how to be great. When they do not behave well, they disrespect themselves.

Holding people to higher standards helps them grow and learn ways to be better. We need one another to help us rise. And as a leader, you demonstrate how much you care about them and yourself when things are not as expected or desired. Your power lies in your ability to respond with clarity, confidence, courage, and care.

Besides behavior, boundary-setting is needed when people make requests of you or your employees. Being able to turn down requests for our time and talent is an essential skill for all of us, yet as leaders, it is especially important so we can demonstrate it for others. People make all sorts of requests for our time. We do not control what people ask of us. They can make any request they like. We must learn to pause before responding to a request for time, energy, money, staff, time off, etc. and consider the consequences of agreeing. What is the cost of doing this? If you say yes to this, what will you be saying no to?

Your power lies in being able to say no to requests that are not in your best interest, not an effective use of your time, or not aligned with your priorities. Pausing to give yourself time to think is the first step. Assess what would work best for you and consider the consequences of responding affirmatively or turning them down. Then muster the courage to speak your truth.

You can say no with grace and respect. As you turn the request down, be sure not to make the person feel wrong or bad for asking; simply state your truth. And don't apologize! (You are doing nothing wrong.) Simply state that you are unable to take on any more projects and that you have stopped doing things that are not your responsibility or not in your best interest (or whatever fits the situation). If you can, refer them to someone who can help them, or show them how to do it for themselves.

People often find it very difficult to turn down requests for their time. Just because you can do something does not mean you should. The highest level of respect you can give is the respect you show yourself. People often say that you must give respect in order to get it; in order to get it, you must give it to yourself. As you treat yourself with compassion and love, you teach others how you expect to be treated, and by raising your standards, you permit others to do the same.

Recently I was speaking with a saleswoman about purchasing the services of her company. We were arranging a phone call with the account manager, and she suggested a time in the evening. I was surprised at how quickly I responded no! I do not (typically) work in the evenings or on weekends, and we found time later in the week. That is a clear boundary for me at this time in my life.

People do what they do. They will offer things; they will make requests. You have no control over what other people ask of you. Other people will have different priorities. In the example above, this saleswoman wanted the sale. But I get to control when, if, and what I purchase and what time of day I take work calls.

What I did need, however, was clarity around my priorities, courage to stand up for myself and my personal goals, and boldness to actually take action on what I wanted and what is best for me given the life I am living and creating. I want space in the evenings for other things. There was no rush for this call to take place, and I enjoy my time after work walking my dog and relaxing with my husband. My priorities were clear, and I was able to use that clarity to make the decision easily and effortlessly.

Of course, not all decisions are that easy or simple. I might have made a different decision if I did not have time later in the week or if I really did need to speak with her sooner. We must weigh all the things going on in our lives to ensure we are following our hearts and values.

The saleswoman had no idea what my priorities are. Nor does she have knowledge of how I structure my days, my schedule, or how quickly I might want to get started with this company. There is a pace to life. You can have everything you want that you are willing to work for, just not all at the same time. Find a pace that works for you and treasure and defend it. Extending your boundaries helps you maintain structure to your life, creating peace and nurturing a pace that works for you and your well-being.

How do you turn down your boss? Perhaps you don't. Perhaps instead you share with them your current responsibilities and how adding that project to your plate would change your ability to meet other deadlines. Do not assume your boss remembers everything you have on your to-do list. If the boss consistently asks you to do things outside of your lane, then it might be time to have a candid conversation about your job expectations.

Boundaries require that you have open, honest conversations, whether it is about someone's behavior or about how you are spending your time and energy. Having a boundary is not enough without communicating it to people when they cross that boundary. If no one knows it exists, you cannot expect people to treat you in accordance with it.

Communication is a crucial part of leadership. Effective leaders know that how they communicate, what they communicate, and when they communicate will help them lead others. Without effective, clear communication, people flounder. It's stressful when people are not clear about what they should be doing or where they are going. Clear, effective communication helps reduce friction, minimize misunderstandings and conflict, and decrease stress, making it easier for productivity to flourish.

In the next chapter, you will learn yet another way leaders care about others—by appreciating them.

CHAPTER 8

Lead with Appreciation

> *There are two things people want more than*
> *sex and money—recognition and praise.*
>
> —MARY KAY ASH

During a conversation with a C-suite team, we were discussing accountability and feedback when one of the senior leaders shared that, since everyone was so busy and they were so short-staffed, she had instructed her leaders not to take time to provide praise or positive feedback. I must admit, I was so taken back that I struggled to maintain a straight face.

Since then, however, I have heard similarly from several other leaders that they had moved away from taking the time to acknowledge their staff or offer praise or positive feedback. Some even said that they struggle to provide positive reinforcement since, after all, the person is doing what they were hired to do.

Ouch.

Unfortunately, people tend to be stingy with recognition and praise. Whether they believe it takes too long or do not see the importance of it, people do not give enough acknowledgment, positive reinforcement, and praise.

A lot of research has been conducted on the importance of positive feedback and letting people know how important they are to the organization. Not receiving positive feedback contributes to greater stress at work. When you never receive praise or positive feedback, how do you know if you are doing good work? When you are not recognized for your work, not provided with development or advancement opportunities, not valued as an individual for the contributions you make, or when someone else takes credit for your work, you may feel taken for granted. It feels bad to work in that workplace. You might feel ignored or invisible. Without each person showing up every day in the way that they do, without their contribution, your organization would not be performing as it is.

Providing feedback, showing appreciation, and recognizing individuals and teams for their work is a powerful way to show people you see them and to acknowledge their importance to the organization. When you do not do this enough, you miss the opportunity to build goodwill, provide positive reinforcement, and create a sense of belonging that builds organizational commitment. When people regularly hear from you and others about their work, their value, and their presence, they feel cared about, and that leads to feelings of belonging and inclusion.

People need to hear from you! They need to hear words of praise, acknowledgment, and appreciation. Often. And it needs to be specific. Identify the specific behavior that the individual did well and share it with them. As with any other kind of feedback, using the Situation-Behavior-Impact (SBI) or the Expectation-Behavior-Impact (EBI) method can be highly effective, and it's really simple to use.

Isolate the situation (or the expectation), identify the behavior that was demonstrated, and then share the impact of the behavior. For example, "Yesterday at the meeting when you gave that presentation and provided the data to the leadership team, you demonstrated poise under intense pressure. This showed how much you have learned and how you really own that material." You might then ask the person what they thought of how they did. The important thing in using this technique is to ensure that they understand the impact of their behavior. People do not always realize the wake they leave—positive or not. This is the opportunity to share with them how their behavior and presence impact others.

If you are clarifying expectations, then remind them of the expectation, objectively state the behavior witnessed, and explain the impact. This could sound like: "As you know, the expectation is that you turn in this report promptly by the end of day Thursday. When you submit the report as expected, it enables me to prepare for my Friday morning meeting. I really appreciate how considerate you are." Or if they are late with the report, you can state that "when you do not get me the report in a timely fashion, then I am unable to share the information at my Friday meeting with the leadership team. This means I am not able to support our department in advocating for our financial needs as I do not have the necessary information. What gets in the way of your being able to provide that report as requested?"

People want to be great! They want to do remarkable things and take part in teams that are doing great things. Often, however, they do not know how to be great, or they do not know how great they are. You get to show them how by providing regular acknowledgment of their work.

Providing feedback only when it is negative or critical creates an environment that incites fear and trepidation, which induces the stress response. How do you want people to feel when you call them into your office?

I remember asking one of my nurses to see me when she arrived on campus. There was a project I wanted her to oversee. She told me when she arrived that she felt like she was being called to the principal's office! We laughed at the time; however, I knew then that I needed to change that perception of my office. While typically I would go out to see the person in their work environment, there were times when my office was a better place to meet. I wanted people to feel comfortable, engaged, and curious if I asked them to see me, not fearful—never fearful. We were a team; I wanted my office to represent an extension of the team and a safe, private space to have important conversations.

Creating a positive and healthy workplace requires that people feel good about their work and feel challenged, respected, and cared about. The work environment is about how people feel at work, which means leaders must consider other people's feelings—how it feels to do that work, to be in that position, given both the context and the individual's uniqueness (qualities, strengths, personality). This is empathy—the ability to step into the world of another person and see the world as they see it. How might they be feeling?

Consider when you have received acknowledgment, appreciation, or praise at work. How was it delivered—publicly or privately? And was that appropriate given the context? How did it feel to receive those comments? Consider how it felt for you when you did not receive any positive feedback. How did that feel? How motivated were you? How did that make you feel toward your leader or manager? What might you do to give more positive affirmation at work (or at home or elsewhere)?

People Matter

For my dissertation, I read hundreds of research articles on employee outcomes including job satisfaction, employee engagement, and employee well-being as well as the numerous factors that make for a healthy work environment. In all the research, appreciation was mentioned as a key factor for job satisfaction. People want and need to be appreciated. They want to be valued. And they need to know that they matter.

When I learned that a fellow nurse—I'll call her Josie—that I had worked with for many years was looking for a new employer, I called and offered her a job. I had the team interview her first, so they could make the final determination as to whether she would be a good fit. They were excited to have her join the team. Prior to her arrival, I called Josie to prepare her for the culture and to inform her that this would be a different experience from what she was accustomed to. The facility where we had previously worked together was pretty toxic. The scheduler, for example, would yell at people and use her power to make people's lives miserable by manipulating when they could take time off. This person had too much power for that position. This was just one example of many where leadership was ineffective and demonstrated their lack of care for their employees. It was a hard place to work.

The staff at this new employer were going to love Josie. She would be valued and appreciated. She would have her needs for equipment, training, support, and resources met. We worked together to ensure she had a schedule that worked well for her and met our needs as well. I wanted to prepare her for this new culture because it would feel so different from where she worked previously. She did not quite understand until she started to work for us. Josie admitted later that it was, indeed, a culture shock!

Being kind costs nothing. Appreciating people for who they are and for the work they do costs nothing, only that you take the time to acknowledge and recognize people for their contributions. You may have to go out of your way to ensure you communicate and are heard. Often, we look at what people do wrong and provide constructive feedback (or criticism). What we really need to be doing as leaders is recognize, appreciate, and share with people what they are doing well. Let people know how important they are to the team, that what they do and who they are matters a great deal to the success of the organization as a whole. You cannot succeed without the people who do the workday in and day out.

One of the fiction authors I enjoy reading is Michael Connelly and his Harry Bosch detective series. Bosch's mantra for solving difficult and even cold murder cases is that everybody matters, or nobody matters. It is not about the title you have, the accomplishments you achieve, the money you accumulate, your status or socioeconomics—YOU matter. People matter. Everyone matters.

People disengage from their work when they do not feel that they matter, when they feel they are taken for granted, used, and not cared about as a human being. Without the human connection, when the focus rests solely on productivity, people feel like cogs in a wheel. People are not machines. Your job is to ensure that people are seen and treated as individuals who make a difference by showing up every day and giving their all to the job. Work provides an opportunity for people to perform tasks, to think, to experiment, and to create. People want to be acknowledged for their contributions and understand how their presence impacts the larger organization. They want to be trusted, encouraged, developed, stretched, and supported.

They need to hear how good they are, how they are appreciated and needed for the success of the endeavor. People often struggle to hear compliments; they are accustomed to hearing the negative stuff, and our brains are wired to notice problems, what might be wrong or bad. They might initially shrug positive comments off. But if you cannot hear compliments, how do you know when you are doing well? How do you know what actions to continue, what to stop, and what else you might want to start doing to help the team? Part of your role will be to ensure that when you do provide positive appreciation and accolades, they are received and heard.

Tell people how you appreciate them and specifically identify what it is about them that you appreciate. Speak with them privately when appropriate and publicly when possible. We used to acknowledge people via email to the nursing group with YOU ROCK when they did something that stood out or helped the team in some way. For example, they could have dealt with a difficult patient or family. We (the leaders) would find reasons to celebrate and acknowledge our staff. And once we started doing that—calling people out and recognizing something amazing they did—other people started doing the same thing. It was contagious! And fun. And it brought people joy. A little joy went a long way given the particularly challenging and difficult work we did caring for behaviorally, emotionally, and intellectually challenged adolescents.

There is a distinction between what people do (their actions or behaviors) and who they are (qualities they espouse). For example, you might compliment someone on a report they submitted. This is appreciating something they do. Explaining to that person the impact their timely and thorough reports have on you and the organization speaks to who they are as a person—conscientious, dependable, and detail-oriented. Both types of appreciation are important.

People want to hear praise and positive reinforcement from their leaders, not just their peers. Make appreciative statements a priority and find time to look for the good in those around you, not just people who report to you. Upper managers appreciate acknowledgment as well. As you express appreciation, others will follow your lead and start to look for the good in one another. Ensure that everyone matters and that they know just how they matter to the team and to you.

Connect

Getting to know other people on a personal level is an important part of leadership. Who is this person beyond the job? What are their interests? What are their strengths, aspirations, or areas for development? In what ways might they want to grow?

People want to know you care about them beyond their delivery of work but let them decide what and how much to share. Some people may not want to share anything about their life outside of work, and that is perfectly acceptable. But many people want you to know they have an ailing parent or an autistic child or that they are involved in a competitive sport. Someone may be working toward a degree that could impact their work in the coming years. How might knowing that help you strategically?

One of my staff was studying for his master's in business administration, and we discussed how he might want to advance in the future. This informed me of his interests so that I could give him stretch assignments to help him grow and develop. Other nurses were working toward their nurse practitioner certification, which meant that once they graduated, they would move on to practice with their higher level of education.

What might be going on in their lives—that they might be willing to share—that you can celebrate or honor? People have children, parents, interests, hobbies, even side hustles. You might not want to get too involved in their personal lives, but they still have them. And if you know they like scrapbooking or soccer, you can be interested in them and ask how something is going, which offers you ways to connect and to demonstrate you care about them.

One of the mistakes ineffective leaders make is to focus solely on tasks and getting stuff done. While results are important, *how* you achieve those results is also important. We know leaders who leave a tornado in their wake. We know leaders who rule with fear and detachment (we cannot really call that *leading*). We know leaders who do not care that you have a life outside of work and some who do not want you to have any interests aside from work.

We also know leaders who make us feel good about showing up every day, doing good work, and being part of something greater than we are as individuals. They know we have lives outside of work, and they care whether we are happy or managing successfully whatever might be happening in our lives. Connecting with the human behind the work is what makes leaders great and makes us want to follow them. Effective leaders help us feel good about who we are and what we contribute to the success of the team. They respect that we are more than just employees; we play multiple roles in our lives and must find ways to manage all of them.

As social beings, we are wired for connection. Without it, we hurt. We have an innate need to belong and to feel included. We need to be seen and acknowledged, to be known, and to matter. Effective leaders understand this innate human need and get to know people. Without connection, there is an increase in loneliness and disengagement. The surgeon general of the United States recently reported that there is a loneliness epidemic.[38] Connection and community are essential for workplace mental health and well-being.

In my dissertation research on the qualities that make for a healthy work environment, community, collegiality, and feeling part of something greater than oneself was recognized as a top requirement.

People need other people to care about them; they need to be needed and included. Leaders can play a crucial role in ensuring that people get along well together, collaborate effectively, treat others with respect (which we will cover in the next chapter), and work together to produce solid outcomes. Celebrating and appreciating one another are ways to make the workplace fun and enjoyable, regardless of how serious the work may be. Work can be play for pay if we have the right work environment. As the saying goes, if you enjoy what you do, you'll never work a day in your life.

How well people support and encourage one another on the job makes a difference in their well-being at work. Research shows that healthy, positive connections at work positively impact our levels of stress and well-being. Having a best friend at work mitigates a stressful and demanding workplace.[39] It does not take a big budget to make people feel they matter at work. It does take time, effort, and attention. Leaders can find ways to coach, encourage, recognize, and support their staff in ways that reinforce the positive feelings that come from appreciating, celebrating, and caring about one another.

Leaders must balance their focus on tasks and getting stuff done with building relationships, getting to know people, and fostering trust through connecting. And while you might be great at doing tasks at 100 miles an hour, you cannot manage or deal with people that way. Relationships require you to slow down, eliminate distractions, and give your full attention to the human being in front of you.

While many people do their best to multitask, we know it is not really possible. The conscious brain cannot focus attention on more than one thing, so either you are quickly shifting your attention between two or more things, or you are doing one thing automatically by habit and the other using your conscious mind. Or you may simply be focused on one thing and not paying any attention to the other. Research shows that it is best when you focus your attention on one thing and not try to do too many things at once. It is inefficient.

Effective leaders practice active listening. They make the space for people to share their thoughts, ideas, and feelings and have real conversations, not just about the work or the tasks but learning and caring about the human doing the tasks—their hopes, desires, fears, and strengths. You cannot multitask if you are listening. You will miss what is being said. And so much of what is said is communicated via tone, body language, gestures, facial expressions, energy, emotions, and even what is not said.

Good listeners listen with all of their being. It requires presence, focus, time, and full attention. It means slowing down. Much of the training to become a professional coach focuses on listening to explore the whole of the human being with whom we are connecting. It seems so simple, but it takes quite a lot of work and practice to clear our mind and energy to be fully present, open, and available for the other person. And then we learn what to listen for.

When you provide the space for a person to share their thoughts, ideas, and feelings without an agenda; without your own biases, needs, or judgments; without trying to help, fix, problem-solve, or change in any way; it creates the freedom to fully be with that person. You must get out of the way and just be with, listen to, and be curious about that person. You connect in a way that is unlike any other type of conversation or relationship. It is why I love coaching so much—both being a coach and being coached.

Leaders can use coaching skills to connect and to truly hear people. When you enter a conversation, set aside your judgments, assumptions, and any agenda you may have. Pay attention to any biases that might come up. Do not try to problem-solve, fix, or change the person. Helpers are fixers. Many of us are professional problem-solvers. But if you approach your conversations with that type of mindset, you will have an agenda, and that means you may not be open to exploring what the person might really need from you. You might assume you have to solve their problem for them or tell them what to do. It can be difficult to listen from a different lens. If instead you assume they are quite capable and competent, then you can approach them differently. Your approach will be more useful when you help them tap into their own resourcefulness. Your presence and energy will project that, and they will feel both your willingness to explore this with them and your faith and belief in their ability.

Listen with curiosity. Why is this talented, smart person coming to you with this now? What might they need from you? So often, people jump to problem-solving without fully understanding what the problem is or what challenge that person is facing in relation to the problem. What is the real problem here? Spend some time asking clarifying questions. And then, once you are both clear about the problem, what is the challenge here for them? Trust that once you have achieved this level of clarity, options and solutions will flow pretty easily.

Ineffective leaders talk over people. They can function as if they have all the answers. People often leave those conversations without feeling heard or understood. If the leader is multitasking or not giving their full attention to the person in front of them, then you can be sure they are not listening. The listener feels like they do not matter—something else is more important if they cannot give you their attention.

You know what it feels like when you feel heard—really heard. It feels incredibly satisfying to be seen, heard, and witnessed. When you do not automatically solve problems for people, it lets you off the hook, which frees you from the stress of having to problem-solve for others, and they walk away feeling competent, perhaps even more confident. If you do not have the time to pay attention in that moment, when would be a suitable time to have the conversation? What does it say about you if you try to multitask while someone is attempting to speak with you? What is the experience you want people to have of you?

Appreciate Differing Perspectives

Have you ever been told you were wrong for feeling a certain way or for expressing an opinion that was contrary to the beliefs of others? How did it feel? It's happened to each of us at some point, and no, it never feels good to be made wrong for thinking a certain way. You feel as though you are being judged and not accepted for who you are. It

Here are three things to consider:

1. Everyone is right in their own minds. Given the information they have right now, their background, experience, and education, they have formulated certain conclusions, and to this person, those conclusions make sense. They have the right to think the way they do. Hopefully, they are open to receive new information so they can learn and grow. They may not be. And that is not about you; it is about them.

   This is an important concept. It is the reason you should not judge prior actions based on knowledge you have today. You made the best decisions you could with what you knew at the time. At that time in your life, you were "right." Your actions had consequences—good or bad—and you learned from the experience. You cannot judge who you were then based on your knowledge today.

   It is the same for other people. They have the knowledge and experience they have right now. That person is doing the best they can with what they know.

2. Language matters. Say what you need to say but in a way that respects and honors the other person for being where they are and for thinking as they do. For instance, you can offer an opinion as a suggestion, "Perhaps you could consider . . ." instead of a demand, "Don't do it that way." Your message will be received differently.

As a leader, sometimes you do need to be direct and tell people to do things a certain way. But even then, tell the person what you need them to know without putting them down for not doing it right: "If you do it this way, then you are going to get the result we are looking for." Providing the reasons behind your request or method helps people understand why things are done as you are instructing. Make sure, however, that you are not expecting them to behave in the way *you* would. Allow people the right to express their creativity and individuality when appropriate.

3. People make mistakes. A good leader recognizes that mistakes are part of learning. The person may lack knowledge or be ill-informed. Remember that in their mind, they are right, and you cannot dispute that. If you try, you will find yourself in an argument. Instead, frame your comments in such a way that the person can be receptive to hear you. Begin the conversation by trying to understand their perspective and their reasons for acting the way they did. Then you can share your perspective or offer new information for them to come to different conclusions.

People do the very best they know how to do at any given moment. Sometimes people need more information, or they need direction. That does not make the person wrong or bad. They are human. Treating them as wrong or bad makes the person feel "less than," the impact of which is to diminish them, perhaps elevate yourself, and create an environment of hierarchy and judgment. This might be received as "I know better than you" and translates to "You are bad. I am good." And do you know what? This kind of environment feels bad!

By operating under the framework that people are inherently good and accepting people right where they are in their personal evolution, you create space for the acceptance of individuality and for diversity to flourish. You allow people the freedom to express themselves for who they are, and this is the path to creating an environment rich with respect and compassion.

Suspend your judgment and seek ways to understand the other person's thinking. It starts with each encounter—each day, in every way, begin to treat others in a way that demonstrates respect for who they are. Make it safe for them to just be themselves and lean in by asking questions if you are curious about their thinking on a particular topic.

Often people need to be taught how to enjoy and appreciate one another, and then amazing things will start to occur. You will begin to experience an uplifting and positive environment where people appreciate each other and welcome each other's comments and feedback. People inherently want to learn and to grow themselves.

They want to reach their potential; they just don't always know how. By making it safe for people to access their greatness, by learning to wonder about one another, by sharing what we appreciate about one another, and by no longer tolerating inappropriate behaviors, we create an environment that nurtures our success as individuals, as organizations, and as human beings.

Look for the Good

What is going well? What do you appreciate about your work, your colleagues, your organization? Taking an appreciative stance focuses attention on what is going well, what you like, and what you are grateful for. Even when you find yourself dealing with a personality type you find difficult, look for the good and consider what you appreciate about them or the situation: What can you learn from them or the situation? What do you value about them or this challenge? What value does this offer you?

Appreciating someone or something does not mean you necessarily like the person or situation. That is your opinion or judgment. When you remove your bias, opinion, judgment, or other personal attachment or viewpoint, you can zoom out and take a broader view. Appreciation is recognizing what is there to be acknowledged and seeing value in it.

You will not like everyone you meet, yet everyone has value. Everyone has something to offer, something they bring to the workplace. If they are not doing well, even that has value. You might need to learn how to discipline, have difficult conversations, or muster the courage to let them go. Then you can assess your hiring practices to learn what you might do differently in the future. Or perhaps you need to suspend judgment, see their value, and realize that what they offer, the value they bring, is precisely what is needed for your team, and you must grow in some way to accept that.

Each of us has our own stories. People are fighting their own inner demons—feelings of not being enough, not being lovable or likable, worrying about what others think of them, being an impostor, being worthy. We each have some undercurrent of doubt that we deal with and work to overcome. Some people overtly show us their negative self-view by making comments that put themselves down in some way. I was on a call yesterday, and one of the women repeated at least five times that she was bad with technology. And then proceeded to put herself down and apologize several more times in the chat!

People need someone to believe in them and validate their worth. People need to be seen for all of who they are. Leaders can play a significant role in appreciating people's innate human value. We can witness them, see them, and notice them by looking for the good and by sharing what we see. We can use praise, acknowledgment, and validation. We can notice people's potential and hold the space for them to be better versions of themselves. Hold the space for people to be great. People don't always know how to be great. They don't always see their own potential. Support them to be better, not by problem-solving, changing, or fixing, but by being with, bearing witness, valuing, and seeing the human behind the title, behind the wall, behind the fear.

Appreciation is for everyone, not just subordinates. What do you appreciate in your colleagues, your boss, or other higher-level leaders? Have you mentioned to them how much you appreciate that quality in them? The higher up you go, the less feedback you tend to receive. People become intimidated by the title. They assume you know more and think they don't have anything to offer you as feedback. How might you make it comfortable and easy for people to approach you? Demonstrate through your actions how to share appreciation and encourage others to appreciate and look for good in the people they interact with.

Love 'Em Up

*The ultimate touchstone of friendship is not
improvement, neither of the other nor of the
self, the touchstone is witness, the privilege of
having been seen by someone and the equal
privilege of being granted the sight of the essence
of another, to have walked with them and to
have believed in them, sometimes just to have
accompanied them for however brief a span,
on a journey impossible to accomplish alone.*

— DAVID WHYTE

When I began coaching people professionally in the early 2000s, one of my teachers, Thomas Leonard, would say to us new coaches at the end of a training session, "Now go love 'em up." He wanted us to love our clients, love the whole being of who they are.

We need each other to help us explore ourselves, to see what we cannot see in ourselves. Even talents can be hidden from us because they come so easily when we have a natural ability, whereas to someone else they might be quite challenging. You may see more in another than they will see in themselves. We all have patterns and blind spots; we have a tough time seeing the good in ourselves and may minimize or dismiss what we do well. People struggle with self-esteem, and yet if we cannot hear compliments and accolades, if we cannot hear what we do well, when do we get to be good?

Learning to love and appreciate yourself is a good place to start. Celebrate and acknowledge yourself in some way each day. Then you can start looking for what you appreciate in others. Be sure to share what you notice about others, and make sure they hear you and receive the compliment. It's your opinion anyway; it's about you and your experience of them. And they need to hear it.

Additionally, while we cannot control whether we receive appreciation or accolades, we can be sure to do what is necessary to be worthy and deserving of them. We can acknowledge and appreciate ourselves for doing wonderful things and for accomplishments large and small. I remember being honored on a list of the Top 100 Thought Leaders in Personal Development. It was a huge surprise to be recognized in that way! And yet it is one of my most treasured awards. I received that award for doing what I do and doing it well. I loved how I was helping others but did not realize the impact I was having in the world until I received that distinction. Throughout my career, I have been honored and humbled by receiving awards for my work. We cannot always know the impact we have on others until someone tells us.

Who in your life might need to hear how amazing and wonderful they are? What might you do to tell the people in your life how much and in what ways you appreciate them?

In the next chapter, we discuss the importance of leading with respect.

CHAPTER 9

Lead with Respect

When our inherent value and dignity as human beings is witnessed, whether by the Earth or by those around us, it can transform our life.

—Jack Kornfield

We know disrespect when we experience it. There was a time in my life when I was looking for work but was unsure what I wanted to do, so I decided to sign up for some agency work. This enabled me to pick up nursing shifts at different facilities around the area to see what was out there for me and find a place where I might be interested in working.

I took a couple shifts at several addiction treatment centers. On one occasion, I accepted an evening shift, so I worked from 3:00 p.m. until 11:30 p.m. The supervisor walked me up to the floor where I would be working. I was provided keys and received a report on the patients I would be caring for that evening. I then started the process of preparing the medications for the medication pass, of which there would be two—one at dinnertime and the other at bedtime.

The medications were a mess. There were little drawers with labels, but the medications did not match the person on the label nor what was listed on the medication card. The little drawers were in no particular order either. I had to spend a good bit of time organizing the medication drawers for thirty or more patients and sorting the medications before I could even attempt to gather the right medications for each patient.

One of our duties was to meet the patients, talk with them, and write a note on each patient regarding how they were doing. At some point during the shift, after I spoke with several of the patients, one of them said, "Why aren't the other nurses as nice as you?" I did not know how to respond to that. I just did what I could to ensure that I was as respectful and considerate as I could be.

Then toward the end of my shift, around 10:30 p.m., I received a new admission. I interviewed the patient and completed as much of the paperwork as I could. Having never worked for this facility before, I was unsure of all the things that might need completing.

So when the night shift nurse arrived around 11:00 p.m., I informed her that I was unsure what else I might do to finish the admission process and asked if she could provide me with some instruction. I stated that I would be glad to stay a bit longer to help. She looked at me but said nothing in response. Nothing. She just stared at me. Three times I asked her what I might do to support her before I left for the evening, and this nurse said absolutely nothing in response. Can you imagine treating someone or being treated like that?

This experience demonstrated multiple levels of disrespect—from the disorganization of the medications to the lack of respect experienced by the patients and the unacceptable behavior by the night shift nurse. This facility had a leadership problem. We know when we experience disrespect. We feel it.

Microaggressions. Missteps. Failures or mistakes that no one talks about. Unethical behaviors. Hidden messages. Unclear expectations. Favoritism. Many of the things mentioned in this book describing poor and ineffective leadership can fall into the category of disrespect. Disrespect leads to feelings of anger and fear, even shame and self-doubt. It contaminates the work environment and creates emotional stress.

Disrespect often indicates an attempt at self-preservation motivated by insecurity, fear, depression, or even unresolved trauma. It can show up as a lack of courtesy or open hostility and downright rudeness. The behavior people demonstrate to others, how they treat others, reflects how they feel about themselves. It is not about you, although it often feels personal.

What kind of environment would you like to create among your staff and colleagues? How will you define the way people are expected to treat one another? What behaviors will you need to model for others? And how will you address issues when they arise?

To create a workplace that is welcoming and respectful, people need to be able to share when something does not work well. People need clear communication, organization, thoughtfulness, honesty, and feedback. They need to know what will and will not be tolerated. And then they need to see how you manage things when events occur that do not fit with these expectations. The goal is to create a workplace that enables people to be themselves, to show up and be seen and valued for who they are and for where they are. This requires a place where respect for all people is valued, encouraged, supported, and taught when necessary.

Needless to say, my experience as an agency nurse informed my attitude and treatment of agency staff when we invited them to work for our nursing department. They were treated with respect and courtesy and were provided with training and mentoring to be able to adequately perform their duties. Engaging with and respecting agency staff enabled us to be well-prepared while providing the agency personnel with a place they would want to work, where they knew what to expect and could perform well at a minimum level. It was a win-win for all of us.

Respect is the foundation for all our relationships. Without respect, you cannot build trust. Respect demonstrates that you care, and that opens the possibility for connection. What do you need to do to ensure that you respect others—yourself included?

A Lesson from a Psychiatric Institution

*Speak your truth quietly and clearly; and
listen to others, even to the dull and the
ignorant; they too have their story.*

—Max Ehrmann

One of the first lessons I learned when I started working in a psychiatric institution was that everyone deserves to be treated with respect. I believed that if I treated people with respect, regardless of who they were, why they were admitted, or their background, they would feel my compassion and love. I intended that they would respond in kind, and with mutual respect, they could learn from me, listen to me when I needed to provide instruction, and honestly, not hurt me if they became aggressive. They would know that I truly cared about them, that I understood they were struggling, and that I did not judge them or hold this against them but rather accepted where they were in their life's journey. I demonstrated compassion for their present state.

I cannot say for sure whether that strategy saved me in any way, but I know my patients respected me. I often received thank-you notes and appreciation from patients, which provided me with the feedback I needed to affirm that respect was most important in connecting with others and aiding the healing process. People want and need to be seen, and they do not want to be judged. And people who are in a mental institution for whatever reason do not need power struggles or judgment. They already feel bad about themselves and their situation; they often carry shame and guilt. They do not need to hear it from others.

When you enter a mental health facility, you have rights, but you lose certain freedoms in order to keep you and everyone else safe. There is an immediate power differential in a psychiatric hospital, and that can be scary for new patients and make some angry. Mental health facilities are locked; all the units are locked. Staff have keys and can leave whenever they want; patients cannot go anywhere without staff taking them. That includes going to the cafeteria to eat, outside for fresh air, or even allowing visitors on the floor. This power must be acknowledged by staff, so they are respectful of how patients might feel about that. If you are hungry in the middle of the night, you cannot just go to the kitchen and grab a sandwich. You may need to ask, and you may not have a lot of choices with what is available for you to eat at that time.

Biases, assumptions, judgments, and preferences all play a role in our ability to respect others. In a psychiatric facility, if you did not like the reason someone was there or how they behaved, you might experience some judgmental feelings and want to withhold your compassion and attention. Yet as nurses we do not have that luxury. We are expected to treat everyone with respect and kindness to help them heal, so they can be released to a lower, less restrictive level of care. Regardless of the reason for the admission, it was our responsibility to withhold judgment and do our jobs to the best of our ability.

Often patients were angry about their situation or events that had occurred in their lives. They carried a lot of guilt and pain from their experiences, either how they were treated or how they treated others. Many of our patients had suffered some sort of trauma that impacted on their ability to cope or deal with other life situations.

There are humans—the beautiful, amazing beings that we are— and then there is our behavior. The two are separate. The human being has infinite value and deserves respect, love, kindness, and tolerance. Behavior does not. If the behavior is inappropriate, that needs to be addressed and there are consequences for our actions. But the human being has the greatest value and potential.

Humans make decisions based on what fills the iceberg under the waterline. And while we are responsible for the behavior that springs from that, be mindful that much of what lies beneath the waterline is unconscious and unknown to the individual. We each have a responsibility to unearth what drives us, but let's face it, that requires a good bit of work—a lifetime of work, and many people have no idea how to do that or even realize they need to. And some people don't want to do the work of personal development, excavating those thoughts and beliefs, becoming more self-aware, and learning to self-manage. We must meet people where they are, accept it with this level of knowledge and understanding that they are doing the best they can, and hold space for them to grow and advance into what they are capable of being. Perhaps our presence and actions can move them ever so slightly toward becoming better at being human.

A Trauma-Informed Approach

Slow down and allow yourself to
be curious about how others make
sense of their experiences.

—MATT LICATA

Part of connecting is recognizing people's humanity and the universal need to be seen, heard, valued, and understood. To do that, we can practice a trauma-informed approach with our fellow human beings. This means that we appreciate that people have experienced all sorts of things in their lives and that their behavior may be reflective of something they have experienced.

You cannot possibly know what another person has been through in their life. Understanding that people react differently to events helps you hold the space of kindness and support when speaking with others. Sometimes, what upsets one person would not upset someone else because of the support systems they have in place or their level of resilience. Our reactions and behavior are often a result of what has happened to us and how we have made sense of it. Dr. Gabor Maté, author of several books including *The Myth of Normal*, says that trauma is not what happens to you; it's what happens *inside* you as a result of what happened to you.[41] Many of the behaviors we witness are appropriate responses to horrific events. The behavior makes sense given the nature of the experience they went through.

We all have experienced traumatic events. The death of a parent can be traumatic to children (and adults too), as can divorce. The impact of a traumatic event will depend on the child's resources to deal with their emotional responses to the event and whether they have a support system to help them navigate these emotions and talk about the situation, so they can better understand it and make sense of it.

During a recent high school reunion, I learned that one of my classmates had been dealing with her parents' alcoholism and fighting when we were growing up. Another classmate shared that she had suffered from anorexia and bulimia in high school and still struggles at times with food. I never knew what they were going through. I had my own struggles in high school. No one ever talked about this stuff—the real stuff that we were working through and how we were challenged to feel normal in very abnormal and difficult situations.

We have all experienced something that could be considered traumatizing: death, illness, accidents, surgeries, or being bullied, mistreated, abused, neglected, or ignored. People can experience trauma in many ways. Situations occur, and how we interpret those events, the meaning we give them, and the stories or narrative we tell about them are all integrated under the waterline of the iceberg, and we can be impacted by that without realizing how we are holding that event. This is why therapy can be so restorative and beneficial, so we can process the emotions around that event in our lives and understand the meaning we have ascribed to it and how it has impacted and continues to impact our behavior. Then we can extrapolate the lessons, rescript the narrative, and redefine what we want that incident to mean to us in the context of our life today in a way that can support healing and growth.

A trauma-informed approach means taking a step back and considering a compassionate response. Instead of thinking, "What is wrong with you?" or "What is your problem?" (that you would behave that way), you might think, "What has happened to you?" (that you would behave in this manner). Whatever you are thinking as you approach the conversation with someone will influence your presence and energy and how you show up for the conversation. Will the person feel comfortable and safe in your presence, or will they feel threatened by you and close off or shut down? By taking a trauma-informed approach, you shift your thinking to allow for grace and understanding, realizing that people are not always aware of how their behavior impacts others, and they often do not know why they do what they do. (Not knowing that what lies beneath the waterline may be contributing to their actions or reactions.)

Behavior speaks volumes and often tells you what the person is dealing with in that moment. Dr. Bessel van der Kolk, author of *The Body Keeps the Score*, taught that trauma comes back as a reaction, not a memory.[42] People carry all kinds of things, big loads and small scars, that they do not want to unload at work, but sometimes it happens. Our baggage often spills out at the most inopportune times. Leaders must be willing to approach tough conversations with compassion and concern, as opposed to anger or frustration.

What does all this mean for you as a leader? Trauma occurs at work too. Many people experience some type of workplace trauma in their career such as verbal, economic, or physical abuse, or bullying by another employee. Some workplaces experience violent episodes. Even in a psychiatric hospital, where violence is expected at times, incidents occur that are extremely violent and unsettling. This is one of the reasons staff process together after every violent encounter.

The story I told at the start of chapter 2 about Beatrice, the boss who yelled at me, was a traumatic event. It was also a pivotal moment in my life that I was able to learn from and that would chart my course into studying leadership and developing stronger, more effective leaders. Not every event results in post-traumatic stress; they can also result in post-traumatic growth.

The stories we've remembered the longest and those where we experienced strong emotions are often the ones we can recall with great clarity. If telling the story still evokes emotion, it means we have yet to clear that emotional energy. We have not yet healed in some way. It's not good or bad, right or wrong—it means we still have work to do.

Every person you meet has their own story. People can also carry generational trauma, as parents and grandparents who have faced significant events teach their offspring in ways that perpetuate the fear or beliefs they adopted from their lived experiences. Immigrants have stories; so does every veteran who has witnessed combat; anyone who has witnessed violence, accidents, or even a natural disaster such as a hurricane or tornado; survivors of a house fire; the secretary whose husband just ran off with her best friend and emptied their bank account; the colleague with cancer; the CEO whose husband died suddenly from a massive heart attack. Events like these happen all the time. And while you don't need to know the details of the person's life, nor do you need to hear their stories, you will need to know how to navigate conversations when the emotions spill out at work and the challenges of life bleed into the workplace.

Being trauma-informed has been likened to using universal precautions in healthcare (e.g., wearing gloves to treat every person as if they were potentially infectious). Treat everyone as if they are carrying some sort of hurt or pain or trauma. Assume they are either carrying something from their past or dealing with something in the present. Approach them by addressing the person behind the behavior or emotion. Are you OK? What is happening to you here? What supports or resources do you need? How can I help?

One of my nurses became unusually quiet and withdrawn. She became very businesslike and impersonal. It was not good or bad, right or wrong (no judgment). She was still performing adequately, but it was different behavior for her, and we noticed. When I approached her to see if she was OK, she told me that her son had just been diagnosed with autism, and she was dealing with what that would mean for raising him. I thanked her for trusting me with that information. She was worried about how she and her husband would navigate this. I acknowledged that it must be challenging (validating her emotions). I asked her what she needed; I did not assume anything. Once she gave me permission to do so, I was able to connect her with an expert who could provide her with information and support. I encouraged her to inform me if there was anything she needed from us to support her.

When people behave in ways outside of their norm, if they behave badly, do not meet expectations, or demonstrate strong emotions, lean in—don't run away. People need you to care. And yes, it takes some time and effort. But it is so worthwhile to care about people and what they might be going through. They do not need you to fix things for them. You do not need to approach the conversation with solutions to someone else's problem. Nor will they find it helpful if you turn the conversation around to talk about your life difficulties. Lean in, ask them about what might be going on for them, and then be silent and give them space to respond in whatever way feels comfortable. If they do not wish to share, that is fine. If they need help, offer access to your employee assistance program, or refer them to human resources to learn how they can obtain assistance.

Many managers are scared to have these crucial conversations because they are not skilled at dealing with their own emotions or the emotions of others. It is important to recognize when you become emotional so that you can process those emotions in a healthy and productive way. If you cannot compartmentalize and put your emotions on a shelf for a moment to address the person, then wait. Take the time you need to be able to approach the person neutrally and without emotion. Your calm approach and compassionate demeanor will demonstrate that you care about them. It is not the time to process your own emotions when you are attempting to address the emotions and behavior of someone else.

When people behave badly, you may feel angry, hurt, embarrassed, or dismissed. And yes, you will need to process those emotions. Your emotions inform you of what actions you might want to take, but that is when you must pause before reacting so that you can choose your response. When you pause, you can step back and realize that it's not personal. It is not about you; it's about what they might be carrying.

As a caring leader looking to connect with others' humanity, look beyond the behavior and into the human being—what might be troubling them? What are they carrying? In the workplace, we still must hold people accountable for their behavior, but we can approach them with humility and compassion. Forgiveness without accountability is enabling the behavior. First, however, we address the human being behind the behavior. Then we deal with the behavior or unmet expectations.

The iceberg visual helps demonstrate that what we see above the waterline are the behaviors, skills, and outcomes; humanness and frailty are things that exist beneath the waterline. They are not visible, but we know they are there.

Most of the time, people know when they mess up. They can feel when you are displeased or unhappy with them in some way or when they have done something wrong. When they are confronted about the behavior, they may become fearful and defensive. Their walls of protection may go up, and their fight-or-flight mechanism might kick in. Or they may break down and cry. It's all OK. This is what people do. It is all part of being human at work. We are not robots. You do not have to be perfect at this; you just have to respect where they are and what they might be experiencing in the moment. You do not need to fix it, change it, or make it all better. Life hurts sometimes. But feeling those emotions is cathartic and essential for healing.

When you approach people with care and concern for their well-being, you are better able to decrease the threat level. When making a mistake or doing something wrong is treated with compassion and understanding, people feel more comfortable being themselves. When you care and connect with the human beneath the waterline, you give them permission to be where they are, and yet you hold that space for them to be better versions of themselves, holding them to higher standards.

When a person's fear goes down, they can access their power, possibility, creativity, and intelligence. They are less stressed, which enables them to think more clearly. That impacts the bottom line with decreased turnover and increased retention, engagement, innovation, and productivity. And that reduces your stress as well.

Safety at Work

Safety at work includes both physical and psychological safety. Physical safety at work enables people to be free from workplace injury or at least limits the possibility for workplace injury or illness. This includes safety from threats, bullying, and other forms of violence in the workplace.

Psychological safety emphasizes the right of the individual to safely be themselves, to be free to make mistakes without retribution or shame, to be able to learn and grow and be challenged by their work, and to be able to speak up and be heard. Dr. Amy Edmondson coined the term *psychological safety* in her book titled *The Fearless Organization,* and much research has been conducted on this concept.[43]

Ultimately, we want people to come to work bringing their full selves. This requires we create a work environment that allows for errors and mistakes. How you manage mistakes and difficulties at work demonstrates your commitment to being vulnerable, being human, and being OK to fail sometimes. Expect the best of people, but when people mess up, make it an opportunity to learn and grow, often referred to as *failing forward.* You will fail; show others how to handle failures and missteps with grace.

People want to be validated when they express ideas and acknowledged when they do good work. If they perform in a way that is not as expected, how that is communicated to them makes a substantial difference. People do not want to be talked down to or bashed because they made a mistake. They already feel bad about it. When you treat people with respect, encourage sharing of negative information, and then handle that information well so that you can correct course, people show up differently. Psychological safety enables people to express themselves as individuals. It opens possibilities for creativity and innovation since people are not fearful of repercussions if things do not work well.

You are a role model for good behavior. End gossip, bullying, or any other kind of disrespectful speech. Address any negativity. Look for the positive in people and situations. Appreciate people and show

how you value them. Redirect negative and unprofessional behavior. Set a good example.

Some people state that they are different when they are home versus when they are at work. A lot of energy goes into being different and adapting to fit different situations rather than being who you are naturally. Think about that and consider who you want to be and what values are important to you—wherever you go. There will be less stress in your life when you can be who you are wherever you are without trying to pretend or shape yourself (or shrink) to fit the environment.

Personal development exists on a continuum. As you learn and grow, you advance along your continuum. You learn to see more and understand more. You can compare yourself to where you were last year, or the last decade, and where you would like to be next year. Do not compare yourself to others; they are traveling on their own journeys. Some people will be further along, and others will not be as advanced as you.

You can create psychological safety by respecting where people are on their continuum of personal development. Meet them where they are on their journey by asking questions to verify what they understand, accepting and allowing them to be where they are, and then doing what you can to offer possibilities and provide new perspectives. Making it safe for them to be where they are is respectful and gives people permission to be their best as they are, while still holding space for them to be even better and bolder.

We are always being and becoming. We are always in process. Where you are on your continuum in comparison to others does not matter. Do not assume or conclude someone is more advanced because of some quality such as age, title, or education. You can outgrow and surpass parents, teachers, and even higher-level leaders in your understanding, knowledge, and wisdom. What matters is to meet people wherever they are and not judge them. This creates safety for all people to be where they are and enables them to celebrate who they are and where they are on their journeys.

Respectful Acknowledgement

When a new employee starts, they are provided with their job description, a handbook, information about the company, and how to utilize information technology (IT). Hopefully, someone will deliver instructions to help them learn their job and understand their responsibilities. Feedback is provided to inform the individual of what they are doing well and when they miss the mark and do something not as well as expected.

Feedback does not stop once they get a handle on their job duties. Continuing to have conversations with that employee to see how they are doing, what is going well, and what challenges they may have offers the leader the opportunity to stay connected and to care about the person at work. It gives you the chance to learn about frustrations you can help with to reduce friction and stress for your team. It is also a wonderful opportunity to get to know that individual personally. What are their goals? What would they like to learn or how would they like to grow during the year? And how might you support them in achieving those goals?

Feedback is a great way to demonstrate that people are seen.

Feedback is often given a bad rap. People don't like it, they don't like giving it, they don't like receiving it, and some don't know how to handle it well regardless of whether it is positive or constructive. Some leaders only provide negative or constructive feedback when something is going wrong. Other leaders avoid feedback altogether. In a recent group coaching session, one of the leaders shared that she only offers team meetings and admitted she does not meet with team members individually, stating that she is too busy.

This behavior tells us that this leader does not see value in meeting individually with her staff. We are all busy; we make time for those things that we feel have the most value—either to us or where we can add value to others. When we state we are too busy, we give our power away to some unknown force. To regain our power, we recognize that we have the power to decide how we spend our time. If we value something, if we see the importance of doing something and it is meaningful to us, we will make the time. It will become a priority.

Feedback conversations or supervision (one-on-one sessions) are opportunities to gather information from your staff regarding their work lives. If you do not speak with your employees individually, how do you assess their work, goals, aspirations, or passions or learn about their challenges? How will you know whether things are working well or whether there are problems to solve and interventions to implement? How will you obtain feedback from your team members on how you are doing as their leader? If you do not have regular conversations with them, how will you learn what they are going through (personally or professionally), what challenges they may be facing, or what they need from you?

Regular one-on-one discussions are respectful. Holding people accountable for the delivery of good work is respectful. It is also expected that you will hold people accountable for the quality of their work. When you do not do this, morale suffers. People will infer that you do not care how people are performing, especially when someone is not pulling their weight or is doing something incorrectly. The impact of quality and performance is felt when your department meets their goals and furthers the mission of the organization and also when people feel good about being on the team. Not having regular conversations with your staff means you miss the opportunity to adjust and regroup if things are not progressing as you would like. You miss the opportunity to learn if someone is unhappy and searching for new employment. You cannot fix what you are unaware of.

Not having conversations with your employees about their work, their performance, the department, your leadership, or their needs, goals, and challenges means you are not partnering with your staff. A partnership requires regular two-way communication on what is working well and what is not. You must be willing to have these types of conversations and create time for them. Some leaders schedule regular meetings with each of their staff members. Some leaders offer some structure for the time together while others leave the topic open for the employee to determine. Whatever you do depends on the context of the work environment but also on the individual. If the individual wants to chitchat or does not readily share about their work, then you might need to guide the conversation with specific questions regarding the person and their work.

There are distinctions between accountability, responsibility, and feedback. Let's define those terms.

Accountability

Holding people to the expectations presented to them upon hire is accountability. We want to be sure that people are performing their roles as needed to further the mission of the organization and do the work necessary. We hold people accountable by ensuring that they know their jobs and are clear about the work as well as behavioral expectations, checking in with them regularly to ask if they have questions or challenges, and ensuring they are well-trained, especially as regulations, procedures, or technologies change.

Accountability is the counterpart to expectations. When you provide clear expectations for how people behave or perform, there must also be a level of accountability to ensure they are performing up to that level of expectation. To do that, we need to find a way to assess people's work or for them to assess their own work and report back. Accountability is the practice of being held to certain standards and ensuring that people will be evaluated on how well they meet those standards.

Accountability is a two-way street. Your employees expect things from you as their leader and hope you will deliver on those expectations. Having regular and ongoing methods for communication enables you to follow up with employees and others on what you are working on, how you are doing, and what you are doing to improve, correct, or fix any problems that have been brought up.

Accountability helps build trust in a team and strengthen the culture of the organization. When leaders hold themselves accountable for what they say they will do, they serve as role models to others and demonstrate that personal responsibility is important. It is as if your actions are making a statement and informing your team and others that you believe in your performance and take yourself and your work seriously. Accountability is a way for people to assume responsibility for their own actions because of external forces and expectations. People behave well and perform good work because of what is expected of them by others. Personal responsibility is different.

Responsibility

Personal responsibility is not something someone else can give you; you take this on yourself. Whereas accountability is answering to someone else or meeting certain external expectations for your behavior and performance, responsibility is owning those expectations for yourself. This is ultimately what you want people to do—you want people to own their work, own their output, own how they present themselves to the world, and own the impact they have on others.

When people feel responsible, they care about their work and their performance because of an internal desire to do great things and be their best. They follow an internal compass of dependability and desire to do good work and do the right thing. Most people do care. Most people want to be great. Generally, people don't rise in the morning and set out to do poor work. People have pride. They want to do good things, enjoy themselves, and contribute to the team—making a difference in their own way.

Some people take on too much responsibility and can take on responsibility for other people's work. This can be burdensome and stressful. While it may fulfill a personal need to feel important, to feel needed, or to feel smart or helpful in some way, it comes at a great cost. For one, it costs you both time and energy. You will not have the time or energy to work on your priorities and your genius—areas where you provide the greatest value. You will be busy while everyone else is done for the day, taking time away from other areas of your life. On the flip side, if you are doing the work, then it lets the other person off the hook. They are not held accountable for the expectations of their role and are not given the opportunity to increase their contribution to the organization. It also does not allow that person to learn, to shine, and to grow and take responsibility for their own work.

If an employee complains that they do the lion's share of the work and feel overburdened, you have the opportunity to ask questions about what this is about for them and why they do not share the work. Having too much self-responsibility is a coachable area for leaders. Be curious about the individual's needs and also what you might do to assist them in handing off work to others, learning to say no, or redistributing the workload yourself. You may need to hold someone else accountable.

Some people do not assume responsibility for themselves and their work. They may go to great lengths to push work onto others. They may not take pride in their work. They may make frequent mistakes and could blame others or not assume any responsibility for their output. They might have values that differ from yours or the organization's. They may lack self-awareness. What is a leader to do?

When someone does not automatically have the internal compass or drive, that sense of personal responsibility, then leaders can use the expected standards and accountability to demonstrate how the person is to perform. Frequent conversations and inquiries about how the employee is doing, what is working well, what challenges they face, and what they are working on help the individual think about themselves differently. Leaders can help employees see how their presence and their actions impact the team as a whole. Leaders can believe in them, offer praise, and inquire as to what that person thinks about their own performance. This helps the individual feel cared about and included and sends the message that they are a necessary part of the team. Hopefully, the individual will begin to see how they matter in the scheme of the team and the workforce, and they can slowly start to learn to take pride and responsibility in how they perform.

They also may not. While others on your team perform at the maximum, some people will do minimal work. You will need to determine whether the minimum is good enough and meets the job requirements. Not everyone will have the same drive to perform at high levels. That is not necessarily wrong. What might you need to accept so you respect each individual for bringing their best to the team—regardless of what that looks like?

One of our new nurses was not performing as expected. We realized within a couple of months that she needed much more direction and specific instruction than what was available daily. Our workplace was not structured with a charge nurse on each shift to assign workload. Each of the nurses had a list of tasks that needed to be accomplished depending on the day of the week, in addition to the regular work of the shift and time of day.

While I did not want to fire her—she was a good nurse for someone new to the profession—she was not a good fit and would not be effective in the role long term. Her needs differed from what we could provide. There was no judgment, just acceptance of the reality of what she had to offer and what we had to offer. If someone is not working out, it's not a surprise to them—they feel unsatisfied, unhappy, or not quite right in some way; they just may not be fully aware of it yet. By being open and honest, you address the elephant in the room directly, rather than dancing around the issue hoping the situation will magically change.

I approached my conversation with her by asking her questions about the work, how she was enjoying it, what challenges she had, and what she felt she needed to be successful at work. The goal was to get her to take responsibility for herself and see that what she needed, and perhaps what would make her feel more comfortable and confident, would be found elsewhere. She admitted that while she enjoyed the work, she wanted more oversight and management during her shifts. She chose to leave us, and we worked out a final schedule that gave her some time to find other employment that better suited her needs. It was the best outcome and a respectful ending. I hope she left feeling supported and cared for.

Conversations are required to create this kind of welcoming atmosphere. Taking time to talk with your employees demonstrates your interest in them and provides the opportunity to share how you believe in them. While you cannot control whether they do great work or mediocre work, you can hold space for them to be great, believe in their ability to perform great work, and encourage them to bring their best selves to work. Conversations with your employees help them see themselves the way others do and reach for more of what they are capable of. Those conversations often include providing feedback.

Feedback

While accountability is holding people to standards and values that have been clearly verbalized, feedback is having conversations to reflect upon individuals' performance, workload, and even enjoyment at work. It is an opportunity to share your views and to solicit the employees' views of themselves and gain feedback about how you might support them. It is a wonderful opportunity to connect.

In their book, *Nine Lies About Work*, Marcus Buckingham and Ashley Goodall challenge certain work practices, including that of providing feedback on someone else's work.[44] The authors assert that instead of feedback, people need attention at work. They need time, they need to matter to someone at work, and they need work that is compelling and engaging to them.

There is a distinction between who you are as a human being and what you do. When we speak of performance feedback, that emphasizes what you do and how you do it. If you are doing something incorrectly, you will need someone to tell you about it and provide adequate instruction. Silence gives the behavior permission. This is feedback. It is also attention. Someone must care enough, have the courage, and be bold in speaking up to share with you how you should do things differently. These types of conversations could happen frequently or as needed. By checking in with your staff and having discussions about their work, you demonstrate you care about them and the quality of their work, and this develops trust and fuels a healthy relationship with the employees on your team.

When it comes to connecting as human beings beyond just our output or work product, the conversation sounds different. It is appreciation for who the person is, the difference they make simply by their presence, and the energy they bring into the workplace. You demonstrate how you value them by sharing appreciation. It speaks to "This is who you are, and we value you as you are." It's not what you do but rather how you do it—your attitude, energy, presence, or other personality traits—things that make you uniquely you and are reflected in how you show up to others. It's how others would describe you, regardless of what you do.

If someone provides you with information about who you are, that is their perception, not really feedback. It is their opinion of you, not truth. This is where the distinction matters. If you do not like how someone else is being, that is your opinion or perspective; it is judgment, and that is yours to own. They are simply being who they are. It is the difference between telling someone you like their outfit (the individual chooses clothes that fit well and look good) versus telling them you think they have a great style and always dress well. The first is what they do; the latter is who they are. Even though it is a positive comment (a compliment), it is still your judgment or opinion of them.

This is why we cannot take anything personally. Everyone has opinions. However, when a leader does share their opinion of us or of our work, some people struggle with it because of their relationship with authority. Some people like to please and focus their attention on pleasing the leader, their colleagues, staff, or others in the organization. This gives the leader great power that must be managed carefully. Other people focus on proving themselves—as worthy, good, good enough, perfect, not a failure. When leaders share information, views, and feedback, it's our perspective, and as leaders, we must take care in how we deliver that perspective. We also ask the person how they see themselves, what their perspective is on their work or performance, so as to shift the focus to them evaluating themselves (and hopefully, taking personal responsibility).

We do need to hear how we come across to others, so we can increase our self-knowledge. The view we have of ourselves is very limited. The reality is that often we do not have a clear view of ourselves, and we are not as self-aware as we think we are. If we ask others for their perspective, if they are willing to be honest, it provides us with opportunities to look at ourselves through the eyes of another person. If we are curious about the impact we have on others, then we need to know their thoughts.

You might ask people for advice on how to improve, instead of using the word *feedback*. You could ask for information as to what others think you should start doing, stop doing, or continue to do. What do they see as your strengths? In what ways are people grateful for you and your work, presence, or leadership? What do they see as the value you bring to the workplace? In this way, you are asking others to provide you with a perspective of yourself that you cannot see from your vantage point. Feedback is the ability to gain information about yourself from others. It is not truth; it is a perspective.

If someone misses the mark on a project or somehow does not meet expectations, and you avoid speaking to them about their behavior or performance, what does that communicate to others about your leadership, your values, and your ability to keep people on track and moving in the correct direction? Avoiding the conversation means you have broken your unspoken contract with your team that you will handle conflicts, problems, and challenges as they arise. Avoiding the conversation also does not permit you to show the person how to do better; rather, it gives the behavior permission. As stated earlier, people want to be great. They just don't always know how. They may not be self-aware and often do not know the impact their behavior has on others. Feedback enables you to provide that information to the individual, so they can view themselves from other perspectives.

Leaders often miss the mark in providing feedback by taking a power stance rather than a servant stance. Approach the conversation by assuming this person is oblivious to their behavior or performance and the impact it has had on the team. The alternative is assuming they knew exactly how their inferior performance would impact others and did it anyway. Most people do not think like that.

By carrying yourself as someone who is curious and hopeful, your approach will sound different and will be received by the individual as you caring about them. If you approach them from the assumption that they do not realize what they have done, or if they do know, they may not know how to correct it, it opens the door to a productive conversation. Don't make people wrong. They are right in their own minds.

What people do need is for you to present information on their behavior or performance in a way that is caring and compassionate, so they can receive it well. When we provide information on someone's performance, they may become defensive. We may first ask them how they see things going—do they think they handled that situation well, for instance. They may still become defensive. They may have difficulty hearing anything that deviates from their view of themselves. Sometimes people cannot hear when they do something that is not correct.

No one wants to be wrong, yet we are all going to be wrong at times. No doubt about it. How we bring this to the attention of the person will be important in how it is received. When a person becomes defensive, you might approach that by asking more questions about their view of themselves, their actions, and the impact of those actions. If they become too emotional and cannot engage in a conversation, then you will need to stop and have the conversation at a later time. Once the emotions take over, the person is unable to think clearly to engage in open dialogue.

Employees are hungry for meaningful information from their leaders and peers about how they are performing and contributing, so they can gain insight into how they can improve and advance.[45] Giving feedback to others is giving them a gift. All feedback is helpful, whether it is constructive or supportive. It is all good, so long as it is delivered in a respectful way. We often do not know the impact we have on others until they share it with us.

If a person nailed the project and you provide no supportive, reinforcing acknowledgment, that is a missed opportunity for informing that individual of their value, how they serve the organization, how great they are, and how much they are appreciated. Silence when people do wonderful things can serve to reinforce their feelings of invisibility and may be interpreted as meaning they do not matter.

Creating an environment of regular, respectful feedback requires that leaders lead the way. Ask for feedback in your regular meetings with employees. How do they think you are doing? What might they want more or less of? What do they need from you as their leader?

Make it safe to share about and process projects or team challenges after the fact as a group. Create an environment where people regularly share what worked well and what did not, what challenges were faced, how those challenges were navigated, and what could have been done better or differently. By making regular assessments of the work, individually and as a team, we start to create an open space for people to care about the work, how work is done, and each other.

People can get defensive when the focus shifts to blame or when mistakes are chastised. Instead, make it safe for mistakes to occur, using errors, mistakes, or missed opportunities as lessons for everyone to learn from. Be sure that openness to feedback is viewed as a value along with listening to compliments as well. People can have just as much difficulty hearing what they do well as they may with hearing they have done something wrong. Be sure people hear the good stuff too. Our brains tend to focus solely on the negative.

Use a Coaching Approach

If you're going to give feedback, it must come from a place of coaching. Most people don't want feedback, but everyone would appreciate being coached on how to course-correct to perform better. Your employees aren't asking you to tell them where they stand; they're asking you to tell them how to get better.

—Author unknown

196

The goals for taking time to meet with each employee are numerous: to offer feedback and evaluate performance, to provide the opportunity to spend time with you, to connect with them and find out how they are doing, to get to know each other, to demonstrate you care about them, and most importantly, to develop them. Evaluating the employee's needs and meeting with them consistently offers them the opportunity to identify strengths and opportunities and set goals for their development.

A coaching approach means you begin by setting parameters and an agenda for each meeting, recapping what has occurred since the last meeting, exploring current issues and opportunities, and agreeing on new action steps and a timeline. What has transpired? What can we celebrate or acknowledge? What actions did you take that contributed to the outcome? What obstacles or barriers did you face, and how were you able to overcome them? Ask questions to go deeper and to learn more.

Coaching is forward-thinking. It requires active listening to explore problems and issues more deeply. What is the real problem here? What is the challenge this person is having in relation to that problem? What are they thinking? What options or possibilities exist? Explore the meaning of the goals and their issues—be willing to go deeper. Ask them to explain or tell you more.

With coaching, take your time to explore the issue a little bit further rather than remaining superficial. When you schedule your sessions, use the time wisely. Having some structure keeps both of you focused on achieving an outcome.

At the end of the conversation, ask what was valuable for them— how this was helpful or valuable, what action steps they will take, and what support they might need from you.

Developing your staff takes time and attention, yet it is worth it. Employers who provide opportunities for dialogue and development find their employee satisfaction and engagement increase. People want to improve. They want to do great things, and leaders must be willing to help employees learn more about themselves and develop and advance their skills to increase productivity and unleash talent and potential.

Leaders do many things: direct, challenge, investigate, strategize, delegate, support, consult, mentor, and teach. Coaching is yet another tool for your leadership tool kit.

Respect Power: Give It Away!

Nothing about me, without me.

—AUTHOR UNKNOWN

Some people cringe at the word *power*, and yet, regardless of where you are in your life or leadership, you have power. You have power to choose your thoughts, beliefs, actions, and response to your emotions. You have a lot of power.

Power is not the problem. In fact, we need power to help fuel our confidence in making decisions that honor ourselves and advocate for others.

People say that power corrupts. It *can* corrupt when people use their power to further a personal agenda. They may even disrespect others who they perceive as being less than. They begin to judge others by what they have and compare that with what that leader has achieved. When this happens, when the effort at ego satisfaction grows larger than the leader's desire or value to do good in the world, then power can be misused.

When you lack self-awareness, when you forget your values, when you allow your ego to lead, and when you become seduced by power and start making choices that do not honor yourself or those who depend on you, then power can corrupt. We have heard that with great power comes great responsibility, and this is true. With power comes responsibility. We must accept and embrace the authority granted us by accepting the position we find ourselves in. This is why we are often asked to take oaths when serving in public office or obtaining a professional license.

Learning what power and authority you have to make decisions will be important when you rise in leadership. As you gain more information, you learn how to best use the power you have for the betterment of the department. Finding your power within the role may take some time. You learn to find your voice so that you can be a person of influence and advocate for what you believe in and for what your department needs. As you rise in leadership you gain more power, more information, and more responsibility, and again, you need to learn how to best use the power you must do good for the organization.

It comes down to honoring your integrity, who you are and who you choose to be in any given moment. You mustn't forget who you are and what you stand for. When you forget, when you lose your moral compass, then yes, you can find yourself abusing your power instead of using it wisely. But remember, power itself is good, helpful, and important; it enables us to do great things and accomplish worthy goals. It is what we choose to do with our power that can either make a positive impact in the lives of others or hurt the very people we serve through the misuse of our power for personal gain. Either way, you have a choice, and that itself is powerful.

Using power wisely means including people in decisions that affect them. Many times, people make decisions, create elaborate plans, and start implementing them without ever asking the people who will be using the product or equipment for input. Numerous examples exist in healthcare, in particular with the implementation of electronic health records and even the purchase of expensive medical equipment without any input from the people on the front lines who will be using that technology. "Nothing about me, without me" is a good rule of thumb to ensure you are including people that need to have a voice. If the project or purchase will impact the lives of others, then include a representative from that group so they can have a voice and provide input. Invite people to the conversation who should be there.

Empowerment means *you* have power, and you are giving it to others. But power should be placed in the hands of the people closest to the consumer or product, those with the most information. If they must go up the chain of command for a determination or decision, time is wasted, efficiency is diminished, and people become frustrated. People feel there is no trust if they have no power to implement decisions that affect them directly. Customers can take their business elsewhere, somewhere they can be addressed more efficiently and promptly. The best person to solve the problem or come up with the solution is often the person closest to the issue.

In his book *Turn the Ship Around*, David Marquet shares the leadership strategies he employed to turn around a nuclear submarine that was performing badly.[46] There had been a lot of turnover, morale was low, and they struggled to meet their objectives for the navy. His leadership gave authority and control to the people and taught them to lead from their positions. In this way, instead of everyone acting like followers waiting for someone else to assume responsibility, everyone became a leader in their own area of specialty and was treated as such. They took more ownership and responsibility for their work and morale improved. They felt valued and capable. Yes, there needed to be a level of competency, clarity of expectations, and clear communication. Once people had developed and demonstrated their competency, knew what was expected, and were provided autonomy to perform their work, they needed only to learn to communicate their intentions rather than asking permission.

One night, a nurse called me after an incident involving one of our patients. She was focused and intense. She proceeded to inform me of what had transpired, what she did, how she handled it, who she notified, and the current status of the child. She then said, "I called you last because I knew you'd support my decisions."

I could not have been prouder at that moment—it still brings tears to my eyes. She did exactly what she needed to do to provide swift care to the patient. If I had insisted on being notified first or being involved in discussions before my staff took action, that would have resulted in a delay that could have been costly for the patient. Yes, I needed to be informed, but in this instance where she had the information and authority to act and was clear about what needed to be done, informing me could wait until the child was safe.

If she had been fearful of how I would respond, if she had not believed in herself and her ability to act without checking with me first, I would have been retaining power that could have and should have resided with the nurse. There were times when a nurse was uncertain of how to proceed, and they would call me to discuss. The newer nurses trusted themselves less and needed to learn how to think problems through for themselves, use their knowledge, and develop their expertise and critical thinking skills. They also needed to learn proper procedures and protocols for different things. I welcomed any phone call to discuss situations to ensure we were proceeding properly.

Since I was not present with the patient, I relied on that nurse's assessment and information to help them make the decision. I had to teach the nurses what authority and power they had to operate at their full capacity (and to the extent of their licensure). They had to learn to trust their own assessment and to make a good decision based on what was best for the patient. By giving permission to this power, I demonstrated that I believed in and trusted them and their abilities.

I never felt like I was giving the nurses power; I would describe it as giving permission to the power they already had because they were licensed and trained nurses. They were professionals and adults. I trusted them. And when something happened where they questioned what to do or wondered what they could do, they reached out to me, and we would figure it out together. We worked together as a team, each using the power we had available to us to ensure the delivery of quality care.

While there will be some power you want to retain, there is still much that can be afforded to others. What decisions or actions might you give away to others? In what ways might you be hoarding power? What barriers do you face in allowing others to have more control over their work?

Competency is so important for building trust and allowing for power and authority for decision-making. In our work environment, there was minimal supervision and minimal access to oversight. So the nurses had to be able to function independently as part of a team that provided care around the clock. We had to be able to trust a nurse's level of competency and judgment.

There was one nurse who worked for us at times through an agency. She would call me regularly to ask basic nursing questions, things she should know. At times she might fail to take appropriate action or fail to call me to discuss an event. This nurse did not instill confidence that she would make good decisions for our patients. I did not trust her abilities, her assessments, or her decision-making, and neither did my full-time nurses. Given our concerns, we wound up removing her from the schedule. If I could not rely on a nurse's skills and could not trust that nurse to do what was needed to provide high-quality care to our patients, then they could not work for us.

In their research on self-determination theory, Drs. Edward Deci and Richard Ryan concluded that people will be motivated to act independently and responsibly when certain needs are met.[47] Leaders are always seeking ways to motivate their employees to perform tasks. These researchers found that when the individual experiences autonomy, competence, and relatedness, feelings of well-being and quality of performance increase. Self-determination is the focus on people deciding their own destiny. It emphasizes what the individual inherently values as a motivating force. The theory postulated that when leaders give autonomy and control to the individual for how the work is completed, when people feel competent and receive appropriate and regular feedback, and when people can work with others and satisfy their need for healthy relations with others, this environment supports people to perform at their best.

Sometimes people just need to know what power they must be able to take action. You may find people asking you questions that may be easy for you to answer. Before you rush in and rescue them, take the task over, or come up with the answer or solution, how might you instead ask the individual questions so they can figure things out for themselves? Some leaders fall into the trap of wanting to fix things for their employees. They focus so much on wanting to help or seem important, but when you step back and pause to help the person think the problem through, they learn to think more critically, become more resourceful, and ask others for assistance rather than relying on you or expecting you to save them.

Sharing power wherever you can pays dividends as you grow your employees, so they become better able to serve the organization. Show people where they can be autonomous and that you trust and believe in them. They will develop greater belief in themselves and become more confident. This results in stronger, more productive team members.

In the next chapter, we discuss how to use empathy to connect more deeply with others.

CHAPTER 10

Lead with Empathy

*Love . . . is the only thing that can liberate
me from myself, from my own self-built prison
walls, from the barriers I so painstakingly
erect. It's the only thing that will assure
me, of what I can't assure myself, that I'm
really worth something . . . A long conviction
of worthlessness builds strong walls . . .
but I am told that love is stronger than
strong walls, and in this lies my hope.*

—CHARLES C. FINN

Connect with the Person Behind the Wall

People hide the best of themselves behind a wall of protection. This wall defends us from the secret world that lives between our ears—all our thoughts, criticisms, concerns, fears, and judgments. Our thoughts are often not very kind, respectful, loving, or supportive. Our thoughts often push us to do more, have more, be more. We compare ourselves with others and rate ourselves based on unrealistic and unreasonable measures. The information that lies beneath the waterline of the iceberg guides us in ways we are unaware of and disconnected from, making us disconnected from ourselves. So we put up a wall to hide a bit of ourselves behind.

We doubt ourselves, don't trust ourselves, and criticize ourselves harshly. We think these thoughts about ourselves and fear what others will think of us. We worry that others' perceptions of us will be equally harsh and critical, that people will judge us and find us not worthy or good enough—because deep down, those are our fears about ourselves. We fear failure, rejection, not being loved for who we are (not being lovable), not being perfect (good enough), and being embarrassed or shamed. Hence, we put up a wall to protect us from what others may think of us and to shield others from learning about how we feel toward ourselves. This secret world is where we live, and it exists under the waterline of our iceberg. People do not realize they are pretending and wearing a mask to hide their fears, nor do they realize they are living behind a wall. This all happens under a shroud of secrecy and mystery.

Now consider that everyone has their own thoughts, fears, judgments, beliefs, self-doubts, concerns, worries, and criticisms, just as you do—regardless of their stature in life, their titles, their accomplishments, their age, their bank account . . . Would knowing that others have internal struggles similar to yours make a difference in how you approach them?

When it is not safe, when a person fears they will not be accepted or cared about or loved, they reinforce that wall. We have all experienced that feeling of silencing ourselves, shrinking, and holding that wall close to protect ourselves from someone who feels unsafe to be around. Perhaps we feel intimidated. Our wall guards us from our mistrust, doubt, and fear of how we will be treated or received.

We have also experienced others who were so tough to get along with or get to know, people who were so guarded that it was difficult to have a conversation with them, let alone connect with them on a human level.

Until I feel that you have my best interest at heart, you won't get all of me. I will hold back. The stress and fear that accompanies this holding back takes energy from being fully present and engaged. A vast amount of potential hides behind this wall. For you to peek behind the wall, to access this potential and unleash the intelligence and creativity that reside there, people need to feel that you care about them as a person.

Connection happens when the wall is softened, when we can get behind it and connect with someone's heart, not their head. We do this through empathy, a desire to know what the person is going through, what they are thinking, feeling, and wanting. Empathy is assessing what that person might be experiencing; compassion is caring about it and being willing to act.

Empathy is often defined as stepping into the shoes of another to see things from their perspective. This is partly true; however, we can never really know what it feels like to be that person. There is no "I" in empathy. Empathy is all about the other person. While we may have gone through similar experiences and be able to relate to them, we can only make assumptions about what they may be experiencing or feeling. In reality, we are different and have different perceptions, expectations, experiences, and stories. All the stuff that resides under the waterline will be different for each of us. So while we may think we know how they feel, we have to ask the person in order to find out what they are actually experiencing. To do that, we must be willing to bring down our wall first and create the space for the other to be vulnerable.

How do we bring down the wall? We have to care. We approach the person, leaving our own agenda, judgment, and ego at the door before entering. We have to be willing to bring down our own walls, be vulnerable, and be fully present with that person without needing to impress or pretend, without attempting to problem-solve or fix. Otherwise, they will feel our wall and continue to hold back. When we approach them without needing anything, with genuine openness and curiosity, we can create safety for the person to be themselves without fear of judgment or rejection. This requires us to be very self-aware and self-observant. In these moments, even if we don't say anything judgmental, if we are thinking something critical, we are likely to show it in the form of emotional energy. Subconsciously, the other person will know it and will continue to hold back. This sacred space cannot be faked; you really do have to care.

Once you enter their space, it is essential that you stay with them in their world, trying to understand them—what they are thinking, feeling, and needing? What is it like to be in their shoes in this moment? What matters to them? What are they going through or experiencing? By remaining with them and not shifting the conversation to ourselves, we hear them, we see them, and we value them—they matter to us, and we care.

The biggest problem with this is that many of us are professional problem-solvers. We interrupt because we know this problem. We move right into fixing, changing, problem-solving, or advising. We judge. Our egos step in, and we want to teach them what we know and show them how smart we are. We must pay attention to these intrusive thoughts as these behaviors deflate the other person. This behavior is a trap—it states, "I know better than you, so let me tell you what to do, how to think about this, and how you should feel." When we demonstrate any of these behaviors, the person shrinks back behind their wall.

If instead we hold space for that person to be their best, if we believe that the person is resourceful and brilliant behind their wall, then we can listen to them, ask questions, validate their feelings, accept them as they are—where they are—and potentially help them see possibilities for being even better versions of themselves. We must stay fully present and engaged, focused on understanding their thoughts, feelings, and needs. We ask questions without assuming any of their answers. If we are able to do this, we experience the gift when the person comes alive from behind their wall.

Challenges to Empathy

As humans, we all carry stuff—thoughts that do not serve us, fears, doubts, and limiting beliefs that hold us back from unleashing our brilliance. One would think that given how much muck we have in our own minds we would be more understanding and tolerant of what others have going on in theirs. Empathy is important for unleashing our potential and connecting with one another, which is necessary for our survival. Our ability to empathize enables us to be fully human and gives others permission to do the same.

In reality, empathy is a choice. We must choose to improve, to take the time and make the effort, to focus our attention, to care, to get out of our own way, and to be aware of our needs so they don't spill into the conversation unintentionally. We need to be intentional.

Empathy requires that we pay attention, and too often we are in our own heads, focused on our own to-do lists and busy with our own stuff. Therefore, we do not pay attention to what others need—what they may be thinking or feeling. In order to improve, we need to choose to put the person before the to-do list. In that moment, we choose to be fully present and curious, actively listening to their words, tone, energy, and nonverbal behaviors.

This requires time, and in our fast-paced, get-more-done-in-less-time world, people just keep moving. As stated previously, you can perform tasks at 100 miles per hour, but you cannot manage people that way. Empathy requires that we stop and take the time to care. We must notice them, be curious and interested, and slow down enough to give the person our attention.

Our feelings about ourselves can get in the way of our ability to empathize. If we are so wrapped up in ourselves, when our minds are so busy spewing negative thoughts about us, we will have little space to be present for others. We will know we have little space for others if we can notice the thoughts going through our minds when listening to someone. Instead of listening to understand and being curious about them, you find yourself thinking about you—what that person thinks of you, that you should be doing something else, fears about not being able to help them, worries about what they may need from you. Or you are thinking about the problem—how might you solve it for them, what needs to be different, and why don't they know this already?

Another challenge to empathy comes with knowing someone for a long time. History between two people can lead to pervasive feelings about them and a preconditioned response to whatever they say. While it is not easy, if you want to be more empathetic, look at them with a new lens. They are new today, different from yesterday—and so are you. Put aside what happened yesterday and be present for what is here today. Tell a new story about your relationship, one that gets you closer to the relationship you would like to create together.

If you are a professional problem-solver, you will listen to people with that hat on and automatically work on finding a solution to their problem. You will want to fix it for them. This is not empathy. This is about you and your need to impress or be right (be the expert) or have the answers. Attempting to solve someone else's problem removes their responsibility for solving their problem and places it in your lap. It diminishes the person and devalues them.

When you jump to problem-solving, you often miss dissecting and clarifying the problem. When you stick with the problem longer, taking time to better understand what is really going on, that clarity itself often brings the person to a place where they can solve it themselves. Once the problem is clarified and understood, what is the challenge for this person in relation to it? And how might you be able to help them figure that out? Keep the focus on the other person, rather than making it about you or making it your responsibility to fix, change, or solve it. This demonstrates your ability to stick with them in this, help them think it through, and believe in their abilities.

Can you ever have too much empathy? Many people are empaths who feel very deeply the feelings of others and are highly accurate in their assessments. Empathy gets us around the wall so we can connect—if they are willing to become vulnerable with us. Compassion enables us to do something to help them work through their emotions and address what is going on for them. If it is too much, we can refer them to other resources that can provide appropriate assistance.

Can we ever have too much compassion? Dr. Gabor Maté stated that "no one gets tired of being compassionate. Compassion is part of our nature, and we don't get tired of being ourselves . . . we get tired of not being ourselves. The problem is not with compassion directed toward [others], but with a lack of compassion for ourselves." We must be aware of ourselves, care about ourselves, and be mindful of what we feel when involved in difficult conversations, which will help us to navigate them appropriately.

Behavior Speaks Volumes

During an informal gathering one night, one woman mentioned how she was trying to find compassion for her younger self. She was surprised by a few of her Facebook posts written when she was younger—seventeen years old, twenty-five years old—and now in her forties, was trying to forgive herself for what she wrote and understand who she was at that time in her life. She asked if we understood what she was going through.

We have all done this: judge ourselves harshly for something we did in the past, stating we should have known better. If you knew better, you would do better. You cannot sit in judgment today for what you did in another time and place. You do the best you can with the knowledge and information you have at the time. Judging yourself in a different time and place with what you know now is not only inaccurate but also not fair or appropriate. You were where you were at that time on your life journey.

As mentioned previously, personal development is a continuum. You travel your life's journey and learn new things, expanding your understanding of the world. You gain knowledge and deepen your understanding of life and how things work, who you are, and who you want to become. As you squeeze lessons from your experiences, you gain wisdom. Where you are on your journey is not who you are;

it's just where you are. Each of us has a different path and learns at a different rate. Our growth also depends on whether we do the inner work to learn the lessons presented to us on our way.

Personal development as a continuum starts with self-awareness. Without awareness, not much is possible. It's why we strive to learn more, so we can see more and be more.

If we extend this understanding to others, we realize that we are all at different points in our understanding of life and our level of personal development. Other people are on their own paths to personal development. So, when they behave in different ways, it is not who they are; it's where they are. No judgment required, but an assessment is needed. If that person is not as aware, not as far along on their journey of understanding, then you must meet them where they are. You cannot expect them to meet you where you are; you are further along—you see more, know more, understand more. They do not currently have the ability to know what you know.

Behaviors reflect what is going on inside us. When you hear yourself use the word *should*, that might be a clue that you are judging and miscalculating where someone is on their developmental journey. It's not who they are; it's where they are. Meet them where they are with understanding and curiosity. And then help them gain some knowledge. Inch them along the continuum in some small way, so they can see more and learn from you.

Many people don't take the time, don't know how, and perhaps don't even know that they need to look beneath the waterline at their own iceberg to learn about themselves and uncover what drives them to do the things they do and think the way they think. It is not easy to look beneath that waterline. It takes work and often requires assistance from others. But change requires that we think different thoughts in order to produce different outcomes. Change is hard because of how the mind works to keep things as they are. In my book *Does Change Have to be so HARD?*, I outline eight strategies for making change easier.[49] You have to be willing to do the inner work of self-discovery and acceptance to be able to see more of who you are and advance along your continuum.

Leaders who lack compassion, emotional intelligence, and humility can focus on the behavior—the tip of the iceberg—and pay little if any attention to what might be going on for that individual. This often leads them quickly to disciplining rather than seeking to understand the person and where they might be coming from.

Leaders who jump right to discipline miss out on helping the other person be their best. Discipline can be helpful when the individual cannot see or does not understand the impact of their behavior or does not want to accept responsibility for it or for themselves. Discipline can be the structure and external force needed to get them to take responsibility for their actions.

If people do not know why they are doing what they are doing; if the underlying habits, thoughts, assumptions, and beliefs are out of their awareness and they do not understand themselves; and if they do not understand the impact of their behavior, then having that conversation to help them become more self-aware is important for their development. And when they resist seeing themselves as others see them, then discipline can support your efforts. Sometimes people don't get the message until they have been fired. We do what we can to open people's eyes to the problem, and we hold them accountable for the expectations we have communicated.

Outcomes speak loudly. People's behavior tells you where they are. You witness the tip of the iceberg. By leaning in and asking questions, exploring the thinking behind the behavior, you can gain understanding of where that person is. This way, you meet them where they are and help them understand more by providing perspective or offering possibilities, so they can think about themselves and the situation differently. Only through empathy, by caring and by your willingness to take the time to help them see more, can you connect with people and help them become more of what is possible. This is how you help others become better, improve, and evolve.

When you care enough to take the time to see things from where they are, you connect. You demonstrate that you care, and the person feels seen and understood for who and where they are, without judgment. You give permission for them to be where they are. It is

OK, even if the behavior is not OK. They can correct the behavior, but who they are does not need correcting or fixing. As a human being, they are just fine where they are.

This act of compassion breeds loyalty and goodwill. People do the best they can with the information, knowledge, and wisdom they have in the moment—not what they might know in the future. Suspend your judgment and be curious. Use behavior and outcomes to inform you of where the person might be on their personal development continuum, and let that information guide you into a conversation about where they are and what they might need to see or know in order to do better. What support might they need from you to achieve different results?

Dealing with Emotions

Inquiry is the precursor to empathy.

—Natalie Nixon

During a leadership development training, one of the participants shared a story about an employee who, at the end of the shift, started yelling and cursing down the hallway. Although this manager was not present for the event, several staff and a supervisor had called her to inform her of it. The outburst occurred in front of staff and patients. The manager told the training group that she was dreading having to discipline this staff member on Monday. This training was on Friday, and the event had occurred the evening before.

I asked the group what they were curious about and how they might coach this leader to be able to effectively address the behavior. What questions did they have for the manager, and how might they support her in this situation? The participants could all relate to this manager's woes. Initially, people jumped right into either commiserating and sharing similar situations they had experienced or offering advice as to how to handle it.

After allowing the group a few minutes to share, I asked the manager whether this was typical behavior for this staff member. She said that this behavior was very out of character. Then I asked, "Is she OK?" Everyone looked at me, a bit surprised at my question.

The behavior told us that something was amiss with this employee. Had anyone reached out to find out if she was OK? No one had. No one thought to call her simply to see if she was all right. The manager stated she could do that after our training. And she could end the call by stating that they could discuss it further on Monday in person.

We are humans first. This human being needed someone to care, to lean in, and to ask about her well-being. What would make this normally well-behaved person suddenly act out in a way that was unprofessional and inappropriate? As a leader, we might need to be careful about what we ask—we do not want to pry or overstep—but we still can care about the person by showing concern and asking about them. We can let them choose to share what they feel comfortable sharing.

This does not mean there are no consequences or ramifications for the behavior. After showing care for the human, the leader will need to confront the employee about the behavior. Expectations for appropriate behavior will need to be revisited. Her response will determine whether further discipline is required or whether placing a note about the incident in her employee file will suffice. If the employee readily accepts responsibility, then there may not be a need for formal discipline. The employee will still need to repair her relationships with other employees and patients. She will need to apologize, acknowledge others' feelings about her behavior, and regain trust.

If the employee does not see a problem with their behavior and is unwilling to accept responsibility for their actions, then you may need to take a firmer stand with discipline and a performance plan, depending on your human resources department recommendations. When you use the discipline process, however, be sure to focus on the behavior and not the person. Use discipline judiciously and respect the person in the process.

Most of the time, people feel bad when they do something out of character or make a mistake. They already know they are wrong and are busy judging themselves, often harshly. What they need is for someone to lean in, to care, to show compassion for the human being, and to provide support and direction for correcting the mistake and making amends. Leaders have this wonderful opportunity to show grace, demonstrate concern, and hold space for the person to be great. They behaved badly; that does not make them a bad person. Respect requires we acknowledge both the behavior and the person behind the behavior.

Mistakes and blunders give you the opportunity to demonstrate who you are as a leader. How might you acknowledge mistakes, learn from them, and respect the fallibility of our humanness? Make it OK for people to be human—for you to be human. People speak of vulnerability as if it is a bad or negative thing. It is a hard thing to admit imperfection. Yet we are perfect in our imperfection. We do not learn from our successes; we learn when we get things wrong. How can we be more open to our humanity?

People have emotions. People have emotions at work. Learning how to deal with emotions is part of being a leader, and the way you deal with them speaks volumes about how you care about the well-being of others. People do struggle with their own emotions. How will you help them to navigate them? Unfortunately, this is the part of leading that takes the most time and requires the most emotional energy. We must tread lightly and carefully, so we respect the individual while also upholding the standards of conduct in the organization. There is a balance here, and yet both are equally important.

CHAPTER 11

Unleash Human Potential

Leadership is a people's game.

We have traveled quite a journey together.

As we know, life is changing at an unprecedented speed. The way leaders have approached leading in previous years, in previous generations, no longer serves the needs of today's workforce and what organizations are facing. The constant change and uncertainty, and the challenges people have in managing it all—including what is happening for them personally—these all require a new approach if we are to navigate through these challenges and create something new. To obtain different results, we must lead differently. That starts with an assessment of ourselves and our leadership as well as the current state of our workforce. Then we can determine how we want things to be different, so we can adapt and change our style to fit the needs of today.

We cannot keep doing things the way we have done them in the past; it isn't working. People are stressed-out, burned-out, disengaged, quiet quitting, disconnected, and lonely. Many of us have lost the spark that enlightens, drives, and ignites us to achieve greater things. We are tired.

To create change and access people's untapped potential and productivity, we need to envision something different. If we want people to be engaged and productive, innovative and inspired, what does that require for leadership? Leaders will need to pay closer attention to what drives and motivates people—individuals and teams—to bring their best selves to work, to be inspired to create and innovate, and to experience healthy well-being and satisfaction from work. If we want our employees to be healthy and safe, that means we need to show up differently and create an environment that supports health, safety, and well-being at work. We start with ourselves, updating and redefining ourselves as leaders, as people with rich lives outside of work and a healthy approach to the role work plays in our lives. We lead ourselves first and show others the way to a healthier, more satisfying, and less stressed-out approach to our lives and work.

We began our journey by revisiting what made us decide to step up into leadership and what we were hoping to achieve. We can reflect upon ourselves today, at this time in our history and ask: what does leadership require of you today, and how might you need to show up differently? The gap between how you behave now and how you will need to behave to create something new is where the development happens. We know that people today require more attention and connection. How does that factor into your leadership style moving forward?

Leadership is more than tasks, planning, strategy, and productivity. It's unleashing human potential. We must provide an environment that enables people to thrive and do remarkable things together to further the mission of the organization. To do that, we must understand people—their needs and how they operate. Through the book, we learned several strategies for connecting with others by first seeking to better understand people. Humans need to feel seen, heard, and valued for who they are and for their contributions; they need to know they matter.

People carry so much emotion and trauma and "mind muck." I introduced the concept of the iceberg earlier in the book to explain how all the beliefs, habits of thought, and assumptions that reside under the waterline are unseen and unconscious to the individual, yet they include all that drives us to behave as we do. When we understand that people are humans first and that their behaviors reflect where they are in their lives, we can greet them with respect and kindness, understanding that people are not inanimate objects; they have a lot of things they are dealing with internally. People are doing the best they can, given where they are in their lives and their level of personal development.

Connection is a key activity for leaders. Understanding the nature of being human enables us to approach others with understanding and compassion. Using the acronym C-A-R-E, leaders connect by communicating clearly, finding ways to demonstrate appreciation, leading with respect, and practicing empathy with each encounter. We can learn to not take things personally when people behave as they do, and we address the behaviors of others in ways that demonstrate our belief in their ability while holding space for them to be human—to make mistakes and to learn from them, to not be perfect.

People need to feel safe at work if we are to unlock their talent and intelligence. When people are fearful at work, when they are stressed or anxious, they hide the best of themselves behind a wall of protection. In order for others to bring down that wall, leaders must provide a work environment that supports and encourages people to bring their full selves to work. That means the actions of team members must be respectful, and leaders set the standard for how people treat one another—they lead the way.

Leading asks a lot of you, yet the rewards are worth it. You have so much power; you must learn to use that power for the greater good, recognizing the impact your behaviors have on others and finding ways to clear the path to make it easier for others to do their best work. By helping bring out the best in those around you, you unleash productivity and potential while improving the bottom line for your organization.

As leaders, we have the opportunity to make a huge difference in the lives of others, in our own lives, and in the organizations we serve. We do not need to stress ourselves out to the point of exhaustion. We must find ways to minimize our stress, think differently, examine our assumptions and approaches to our work, and create new strategies for leading.

While there are things we cannot control, there are many things we *can* control, and by doing so we reduce stress for our team members and for ourselves. We can set clear expectations for the work and how it gets done, which makes it easier for people to assume personal responsibility for how well they perform. We can also hold people accountable for results by providing regular feedback and acknowledgement and being curious about how the individual feels about their own performance.

Leaders can build confidence in employees while decreasing the stress they experience. We do this in several ways. Besides increasing our self-awareness and developing ourselves to ensure we are not the cause of the stress, we can search for and eliminate the challenges and the friction that impede people's ability to get work accomplished. We can also offer praise and appreciation and develop our employees, stretching them to grow and become better versions of themselves. We acknowledge, appreciate, and value our people. We can provide autonomy and clear communication, ensure people are treated with respect, and use empathy to relate to others.

We must muster our moral courage to do the right things, and when something goes wrong, we can communicate, fix it, and learn from it publicly. When people feel safe at work, there is trust. We develop that trust through our behaviors. Addressing challenges and conflict and having those tough conversations with empathy, compassion, and respect enables us to lower the wall that keeps people from bringing their full selves to work. Realizing that people carry a lot of pain and emotions they may be unaware of and that every person has value beyond their behavior, performance, or title helps us remain humble, relatable, and kind.

By approaching leadership differently, we increase our confidence, improve our situations, care about our people and ourselves, and create work environments that support our well-being and the well-being of others. We can enjoy our work and enjoy working together.

If we accomplish this even in small ways, we increase engagement and productivity, which in turn impacts the organization and our community at large.

Please reach out and share with me your thoughts, learnings, and comments about how you are using these strategies to meet the current demands of your employees. Enjoy the journey!

Notes

Chapter 1

1. Almeida, M., and C. Frumar. "Help Your Employees Cope with Stress." Gallup. August 23, 2023. https://www.gallup.com/workplace/509726/help-employees-cope-stress.aspx.
2. Pfeffer, J. *Dying for a Paycheck*. HarperBusiness, 2018.
3. Karasek, R., and T. Theorell. *Healthy Work: Stress, Productivity, and the Reconstruction of Working Life*. Basic Books, Inc., 1990.
4. Pfeffer, J. *Dying for a Paycheck*. HarperBusiness, 2018.
5. Edmondson, A. C. *The Fearless Organization*. John Wiley & Sons, 2018.
6. United States. Public Health. Office of the Surgeon General. *Our Epidemic of Loneliness and Isolation: The U.S. Surgeon General's Advisory on the Healing Effects of Social Connection and Community*, 2023.
7. Clifton, J. *Blind Spot: The Global Rise of Unhappiness and How Leaders Missed It*. Gallup Press, 2022.
8. World Health Organization. *Burn-out an Occupational Phenomenon: International Classification of Diseases*, 2019.
9. Clifton, J., and Sinyan. "Europe Gets Life Right but Work Wrong." Gallup. 2022. https://www.gallup.com/workplace/510584/europe-gets-life-right-work-wrong.aspx.

10. Ryan, R. M., and E. L. Deci. "Self-Determination Theory and the Facilitation of Intrinsic Motivation, Social Development, and Well-Being." *American Psychologist* 55 (2000): 68–78.
11. Lencioni, P. *The Three Signs of a Miserable Job: A Fable for Managers (and Their Employees)*. Jossey-Bass, 2007.
12. Donley, J. *Work Environment and Job Satisfaction: A Correlational Study of Childcare Workers in Behavioral Healthcare*. Doctoral dissertation. ProQuest No. 27668079, 2019.

Chapter 2

13. United States. Public Health Service. Office of the Surgeon General. *Surgeon General's Framework for Mental Health & Well-Being in the Workplace*, 2022.

Chapter 3

14. Acharya, S., and S. Shukla. "Mirror Neurons: Enigma of the Metaphysical Modular Brain." *Journal of Natural Science, Biology, and Medicine* 3, no. 2 (2012): 118–124. doi:10.4103/0976-9668.101878.
15. Scott, S. *Fierce Conversations: Achieving Success at Work and in Life, One Conversation at a Time*. Berkey Books, 2002.

Chapter 4

16. *Merriam-Webster Dictionary*.
17. *Cambridge English Dictionary*.
18. Grant, A. *Think Again: The Power of Knowing What You Don't Know*. Viking, Penguin Random House, 2021.
19. Gallup. https://www.gallup.com/cliftonstrengths/en/252137/home.aspx.

20. Covey, S. R. *The 7 Habits of Highly Effective People: Restoring the Character Ethic.* Rev. ed. Free Press, 2004.

Chapter 5

21. Kegan, R., and L. L. Lahey. *Immunity to Change.* Harvard Business Review Press, 2009.
22. Ruiz, D. M. *The Four Agreements.* Amber-Allen Publishing, 2001.
23. LearningInAction.com.
24. DrJulieDonley.com.
25. Schwartz, T., J. Gomes, and C. McCarthy. *The Way We're Working Isn't Working: The Four Forgotten Needs That Energize Great Performance.* Simon & Schuster Limited, 2016.
26. Donley, J. *The Journey Called You: A Roadmap to Self-Discovery and Acceptance.* Nurturing Your Success LLC, 2005; 2021.
27. Covey, S. R. *The 7 Habits of Highly Effective People: Powerful Lessons in Personal Change.* Simon & Schuster, 2013.

Chapter 6

28. Karasek, R. A. "Job Demands, Job Decision Latitude, and Mental Strain: Implications for Job Redesign." *Administrative Science Quarterly* 24, no. 2 (1979): 285–308. doi:10.2307/2392498.
29. Eurich, T. *Insight: The Surprising Truth about How Others See Us, How We See Ourselves, and Why the Answers Matter More Than We Think.* Crown Currency, 2018.
30. Donley, J. *Work Environment and Job Satisfaction: A Correlational Study of Childcare Workers in Behavioral Healthcare.* Doctoral dissertation. ProQuest No. 27668079, 2019.

31. Donley, J. "The Impact of Work Environment on Job Satisfaction: Pre-COVID Research to Inform the Future." *Nurse Leader*, December 2021. https://doi.org/10.1016/j.mnl.2021.08.009.

Chapter 7

32. Feltman, C. *The Thin Book of Trust: An Essential Primer for Building Trust at Work.* Thin Book Publishing, 2009.
33. Sinek, S. "Start with Why—How Great Leaders Inspire Action | Simon Sinek | TEDxPugetSound." YouTube. 2009. https://www.youtube.com/watch?v=u4ZoJKF_VuA.
34. Amazon. https://www.amazon.jobs/content/en/our-workplace/leadership-principles.
35. Ruiz, D. M. *The Four Agreements.* Amber-Allen Publishing, 2001.
36. Ruiz, D. M. *The Four Agreements.* Amber-Allen Publishing, 2001.
37. Rosenberg, M. B. *Nonviolent Communication.* PuddleDancer Press, 2005.

Chapter 8

38. United States. Public Health. Office of the Surgeon General. *Our Epidemic of Loneliness and Isolation: The U.S. Surgeon General's Advisory on the Healing Effects of Social Connection and Community*, 2023.
39. Patel, A., and S. Plowman. "The Increasing Importance of a Best Friend at Work." Gallup. August 17, 2022. https://www.gallup.com/workplace/397058/increasing-importance-best-friend-work.aspx.
40. Fuimano (Donley), J. "No One Gets to Be Wrong." *Biospace*, 2006. https://www.biospace.com/article/releases/no-one-gets-to-be-wrong-/?s=106.

Chapter 9

41. Maté, G., and D. Maté. *The Myth of Normal: Trauma, Illness, and Healing in a Toxic Culture*. Avery, an imprint of Penguin Random House, 2022.
42. van der Kolk, B. A. *The Body Keeps the Score: Brain, Mind, and Body in the Healing of Trauma*. Viking, 2014.
43. Edmondson, A. C. *The Fearless Organization*. John Wiley & Sons, 2018.
44. Buckingham, M., and A. Goodall. *Nine Lies about Work: A Freethinking Leader's Guide to the Real World*. Harvard Business Review Press, 2019.
45. McLain, D., and B. Nelson. "How Effective Feedback Fuels Performance." Gallup. 2022. https://www.gallup.com/workplace/357764/fast-feedback-fuels-performance.aspx.
46. Marquet, L. D. *Turn the Ship Around!* Portfolio Penguin, 2015.
47. SelfDeterminationTheory.org. https://selfdeterminationtheory.org/theory/.

Chapter 10

48. Finn, C. C. "Please Hear What I'm Not Saying." 1966. https://poetrybycharlescfinn.com/pages/please-hear-what-im-not-saying.
49. Donley, J. *Does Change Have to Be so HARD? Eight Strategies for Making Change Easier*. Nurturing Your Success LLC, 2011; 2023.

Gratitude

This book has been incubating in my mind for decades. How do great leaders lead well? Over the years, I have witnessed and experienced leaders of all kinds, and I am grateful for the lessons learned from all of them—the good and the not-so-good lessons.

There are many people for whom I am grateful for helping me with this book and its development. The people over at selfpublishing. com have been wonderful to work with. I appreciate Scott Allen who has guided me through this process and the folks who helped with book design and production. Thanks also to Robin Reed, my editor, who painstakingly reviewed the book for clarity.

My cup is overflowing with gratitude for the people in my life. Each of you has made an indelible impression. While I will not list everyone, please know that you matter to me, and I love you.

My husband, Lou, patiently listened to me verbalize my thoughts over countless hours. Thank you, my love! My family and friends are so supportive of my ventures; they believe in me and encourage me to stretch myself and share my ideas.

I am grateful for my coach, Alison Whitmire, who helps me access the deeper recesses of my beliefs and habits of thought that reside beneath the waterline in my iceberg to help unleash my potential. Her belief in me and her ability to hold the space for me to access my brilliance means so much.

I am grateful for the many coaches and colleagues who I have learned from, worked with, coached, and been coached by over the years, who have taught me and helped me grow and learn.

I have so much gratitude and appreciation for my coaching clients—as much as they learn from the work we do together, I learn so much from them. Working with my coaching clients compels me to continue to grow and develop my mastery in order to better serve them.

My gratitude and love runs deep for the nurses with whom I have had the pleasure to work over the years. We grew together, learned and supported one another, kept people safe, and were able to achieve great results for our patients. Now that I am retired from that line of work, I am filled with appreciation for the work of psychiatric care providers and so proud to have been one of them.

I could not do what I do without the people in my life, and I would not be who I am today without the people I have met and who have impacted me along my journey. Each person is an angel who has taught me something or enabled me to express or teach something. I feel so very blessed for our paths having crossed.

About Dr Julie Donley

D r. Julie Donley is a renowned expert in leadership, coaching, and organizational behavior with over 30 years of experience. As a professional certified coach, dynamic facilitator, and inspirational speaker she has dedicated her career to helping leaders navigate challenging situations, reduce stress, and lead with confidence and calm.

Julie's passion for leadership was ignited when she entered her healthcare career in psychiatric nursing in 1993. There she encountered ineffective leadership and a toxic work environment which had a profound impact on team dynamics and patient care. This experience led her on a quest to study and develop the leadership qualities necessary to produce a healthy work environment that would enable people to thrive.

Dr. Donley served as an executive nurse in behavioral health for nearly a decade while also providing internal coaching and leadership development, training, and mentoring. She started coaching leaders professionally in 2001 and founded her company, Nurturing Your Success LLC, to provide personal and leadership development for those who want to show up prepared, confident, and authentic in their leadership roles. Through her company, she has positively influenced countless leaders by offering coaching, training, and consultancy services tailored to their unique needs.

A prolific author, Dr. Donley has written several acclaimed books, including *Does Change Have to be so HARD?* and *The Journey*

Called YOU: A Roadmap to Self-Discovery and Acceptance. Her writings combine practical insights with profound personal wisdom, helping readers navigate the complexities of personal and professional growth. Her unique approach focuses on simplifying the complex, making leadership strategies easy to understand and apply.

Her passion for understanding the importance of a leader's impact on the workforce extended to her doctoral dissertation where she investigated the impact of factors of the psychosocial work environment on job satisfaction for behavioral healthcare workers. Julie has been recognized for her work by *Leadership Excellence Magazine* as a Top 100 Thought Leader in Personal Development and has received *Main Line Today's* Healthcare Hero award.

Dr. Donley is an avid learner and holds multiple degrees and certifications that underscore her expertise and commitment to excellence. She completed her Doctor of Education in Organizational Leadership from Grand Canyon University, a Master of Business Administration from DeSales University, a Bachelor (and Associate) of Science in Nursing from Gwynedd Mercy University, and a Bachelor of Business Administration from Temple University. She received an executive certificate in nonprofit management from Georgetown University, and is a certified diversity, group, and team coach as well as a professional certified coach with the International Coach Federation.

Dr. Donley is known for her dynamic, energetic, and fun personality. She is passionate about empowering leaders to lead more effectively, fostering environments of respect and empathy, and achieving remarkable results. Julie is married and enjoys traveling, riding motorcycles, and spending time with her family and friends.

For more information about Dr. Donley and her work, visit her online:

Website: www.DrJulieDonley.com
LinkedIn: https://www.linkedin.com/in/drjuliedonley/
Facebook: https://www.facebook.com/DrJDonley/
YouTube: https://www.youtube.com/channel/UC_oUnKYA
   7Ky0GGeD5UkcdCA
Contact her at DrJulieDonley@gmail.com.

Made in the USA
Middletown, DE
11 September 2024

60140314R00139